ALL THINGS ARE
POSSIBLE
THROUGH
PRAYER

ALL THINGS ARE POSSIBLE THROUGH PRAYER

The Faith-Filled Guidebook That Can Change Your Life

CHARLES L. ALLEN

Revell
A DIVISION OF
Baker Book House Co

Published by Fleming H. Revell
a division of Baker Book House Company
P.O. Box 6287, Grand Rapids, MI 49516-6287

Printed in the United States of America

Library of Congress Cataloging-in-Publication Data
Allen, Charles Livingstone, 1913–
    All things are possible through prayer : the faith-filled guidebook that can change your life / Charles L. Allen.
        p.   cm.
    Originally published: 1958. With new pref.
    Includes bibliographical references (p.   ).
    ISBN 0-8007-5899-4
    1. Prayer. I. Title.
BV220.A4 2003
248.3′2—dc21   2003008294

Scripture is taken from the King James Version of the Bible.

To
my dear friends of
Grace Methodist Church
Atlanta, Georgia,
whose love and prayers have
blessed me during the more than
ten years I have been their pastor

CONTENTS

CONTENTS

PREFACE

Keys for Locked Doors

It is a humbling thing for me to know that hundreds of thousands of people all over the world have been helped through reading the book you hold in your hands. I have heard from many of those readers over the years, and I know this to be true. So it pleases me that Fleming H. Revell has decided to publish this new edition of *All Things Are Possible Through Prayer*.

I invite you to join me on the most amazing road you'll ever travel as we take the best journey you'll never finish! Why do I say that? Because while faith is a simple thing, it is not easy. Rather, it is a lifelong journey for every praying person, young or old, from any walk of life. Together in these pages you and I will discover why we pray, how we pray, and how God answers those prayers. We'll also take encouragement from the experience of others, both in Bible times and in contemporary life. And in the process, we'll draw closer to our Lord.

We are living in troubling times. Yet I believe that with God nothing is hopeless. My wish is that you learn to nurture that belief yourself. To that end, I have sought in these pages to point out some of the locked doors of life and some of the prayer-keys that will open those doors.

Both the faithful and the doubting have taken heart in the words of Jesus: "If thou canst believe, all things are possible to him that believeth" (Mark 9:23). I have lived to see the truth in that Scripture, and I believe that, indeed, all things are possible through prayer.

Charles L. Allen
Houston, Texas
2003

1

THE RECEPTIVE MOOD

It seems strange that Jesus' disciples should have said, "Lord, teach us to pray" (Luke 11:1). These men doubtless had grown up in strictly religious homes. They had gone to church and they had prayed all their lives. A year before if you had asked the disciples, "Do you know how to pray?" they would have been indignant. "Of course, we know how to pray," they would have insisted. "We have prayed regularly every day for years."

They could have quoted you many verses in the Bible in reference to prayer. They could have answered the arguments against prayer and given the reasons for prayer. However, when they saw Jesus pray, they realized they did not know how to pray. They saw how much time He gave to prayer and what it meant in His own life. They saw Him go into prayer in one mood and come out in another. As a result of His prayers, they saw things become different. To them prayer had been a form but to Christ it was a force.

As those disciples saw Jesus pray, they realized it was something quite different from what they had been doing when they prayed. They realized they didn't know how, after they had seen Jesus pray, and so they said, "Lord, teach us to pray." Their request has been on the lips of many people since that day.

In answer to their request, Jesus told them, "When ye pray, say, Our Father which art in heaven, Hallowed be thy name. . . ." That is, the first step in prayer is: you must believe in God, you must center your mind on God, you must feel the presence of God, you must receive the Spirit and power of God into your own mind and heart.

The world is quite familiar with the immortal story of the great Tolstoy. He was wealthy, he was honored, he was acclaimed far and wide, but that did not satisfy. He tells how he ran through the sinful thrills of life but they all left him with a gnawing discontent.

One day he was walking in the country. He saw a peasant and observed the look of peace and happiness on the man's face. Tolstoy said to himself, "This peasant has nothing and yet he seems filled with the joy of life." After a period of honest study, he concluded that he was missing God, and so he sought God. One day he found Him and then he knew the answer to that inner hunger and discontent. As a result of his own experience, Tolstoy gave us this great conclusion: "To know God is to live."

The beginning of prayer is to receive God. That means we must pray in a receptive mood. You get up in the morning thinking of the things you must do that day. Your mind is active and aggressive and hour by hour during the day you spend your thought, time, and effort in your work and activities. Then that night you attend a concert of great music. But to enjoy the concert, you must change your mood. Instead of being aggressively active, at the concert you must become receptive. Likewise, when we pray, we must be receptive. "Be still, and know that I am God," said the psalmist.

The first step to prayer is receiving God. The reason many people never learn to pray is that they never change from an aggressive into a receptive mood. We go along through life saying, "This is what I want—this is what I will do"—and prayer is just an additional way of realizing our ambitions.

For large numbers, prayer is merely a spare tire, something to be used when the other tires fail. We plan, we work, and then, if we don't get what we want and can't do what our hearts are set on, we say, "God, you get it for me," or, "God, you do it for me." We try to make prayer just a continuation of our "go-getting" spirit of modern life.

But in countless ways, God breaks in upon our lives. For example, you get up one morning feeling extra good. The sky is blue, the air is crisp, you feel good, you think of your opportunities of the day. You say, "I am so thankful to be alive." But thankful to whom? Not to the sky—it wouldn't understand your feelings. Not to your family and friends—they mean much to you but they didn't create your world. You are not thankful to yourself. You are expressing your praise, not receiving it. Subconsciously you are recognizing God and you are really praying.

Some tragedy comes into our lives. Our first reaction is one of rebellion. We say, "It isn't fair—I resent this happening—I don't deserve it." But whom are we speaking to? Not to the four walls of our house for they can't hear what we say. Though we may express our thoughts to some friend, we are not really talking to that person. He or she did not cause the tragedy. We are aware of the Power beyond human power that is at work in our daily lives. We recognize God.

Sometimes we feel ashamed of ourselves. Are we ashamed because somebody has found us out? That may be the case, but many times we feel shame when we know we will never be found out. Those who are the closest to us will never know, yet still we feel shame. Why? Because we know it is known. Known by whom? By ourselves? Yes, but also known by Someone else and that Someone is God. God has a way of breaking in upon our lives and making Himself felt.

The beginning of power is consciously opening our minds to God and being receptive to His presence, His Spirit, His voice, and His will. Jesus said, "[Some people] think that they shall be heard for their much speaking," but He points out, "your Father knoweth what things ye have need of, before you ask Him." The object of prayer is not telling God a lot of things. First, said Jesus, pray, "Our Father which art in heaven, Hallowed be thy name."

Really praying those words accomplishes what Whittier had in mind when he prayed:

> Drop Thy still dews of quietness,
> Till all our strivings cease;
> Take from our souls the strain and stress,
> And let our ordered lives confess
> The beauty of Thy peace.

When a person prays with his mind centered on God, two results follow. First, our prayers are positive instead of negative. Time and again some person has said to me, "I prayed but it didn't help." The fact is that often when we pray about some habit, some temptation, some weakness, or some need, it does real harm to us.

For example, here is one who is sick and prays to get well. This one says: "Lord, I am very sick." The Lord may answer, "You don't seem very sick to me." "Oh yes, Lord, you don't know. Feel my brow and you'll know I have a temperature. Feel my pulse—

see how weak it is. Lord, I don't feel like sitting up, anything I eat nauseates me, everything gets on my nerves. Oh yes, Lord, I am sick. Make me well and give me health."

That sort of praying will make even a well person sick. Certainly it won't make a sick person well. The same thing applies to some harmful habit of your life. The more earnestly you pray about it, the more firmly it becomes fixed in your thinking. But when one begins with God, instead of concentrating on his problems he fills his mind with God's power; instead of our sins we see His salvation; instead of our fears in life we find strength through our faith in Him.

Second, when God is the center of our prayer, then we pray without becoming discouraged. The reason we get discouraged is that we lose hope and the reason we lose hope is because we lose God. The Bible says, "Hope thou in God." God has the wisdom to solve every problem, He has the power to win every victory.

Study the Twenty-third Psalm, the finest example of prayer in the Old Testament. There we have nine petitions centering on the character and activity of God. David had problems and weaknesses in his own life. He lived in a world that sometimes looked dark, but in his prayer he is positive. He affirms the existence of God and feels His presence. Then David closes that prayer with two conclusions: First, tomorrow will be good—"Goodness and mercy shall follow me," he says. Second, beyond tomorrow will also be good—for he will be in "the house of the Lord."

Read again the Lord's Prayer. It begins with God and then it looks out on life with optimistic faith. It believes God's Kingdom can come; that our daily physical needs can be met; that our sins can be forgiven; that we can have strength for the trials of life that lie ahead.

Bishop Arthur J. Moore tells of a man who jumped to his death from the window of a high building. Commenting on that man, the old janitor of the building, who knew the man, said, "When a man has lost God, there ain't nothing to do but jump." But as long as one has God, there is always something else to do. No matter how bad yesterday may have been or today is, with God there is a good tomorrow ahead.

And the first purpose of prayer is to know God. It is as Tolstoy said, "To know God is to live."

2

DARING TO ASK

Kate Smith was asked to describe her philosophy of living. She said it had been the same since she was a little girl and could be stated in just three words: *Try asking God.* Then she told the story of the beginning of that faith for her.

Once she was out in a rowboat on the Chesapeake Bay with two other girls. All three were in their early teens. They did not notice that the outgoing tide had swept them far out from the shore and that it was nearly dark. They suddenly became filled with fear. They cried for help but no one could hear. Then Kate Smith remembered a statement in the Bible that if two or three are gathered together in His name, He is in the midst of them.

"We have the limit," she said to her friends. "The Bible says 'two or three' and we have three. God will save us if we ask Him." They prayed. And out of the gathering darkness loomed the lines of a boat. They were taken on board and carried back to safety. From that time on, in trouble, in need, in disappointment, in every circumstance of life, her philosophy has been simply, "Try asking God."

That simple faith appeals to me and I seek to practice it myself. Of course, there are some who object on the grounds that it is using your religion for your own good. But I ask, "Does God object to His children being successful in life?" I have read the New Testament all the way through and I do not recall a single statement urging Christians to be failures in life. And I recall that Jesus said, "If ye then, being evil, know how to give good gifts unto your children, how much more shall your Father which is in heaven give good things to them that ask him?" And in that same passage, Jesus said, "Ask, and it shall be given you . . ." (Matt. 7:7–11). Indeed, why not try asking God?

We read in the very first chapters of the Bible how God made the world. Everything that is here: He made it. Then He made man and He told man to subdue the earth. That is, possess it and use it for his own good. And when I ask God to help me in life, I am asking Him to help me accomplish what He, Himself, told me to do. Surely then, it is not displeasing to God to ask Him for His help and His blessings.

But on the other hand, some will say, I did ask God but I did not receive what I asked. We all remember reading the *Adventures of Huckleberry Finn* and we recall Huck talking about this matter of prayer. He said,

Miss Watson she took me in the closet and prayed, but nothing come of it. She told me to pray every day, and whatever I asked for I would get it. But it wasn't so. I tried it. Once I got a fish-line, but no hooks. It warn't any good to me without hooks. I tried for the hooks three or four times, but somehow I couldn't make it work. By and by, one day, I asked Miss Watson to try for me, but she said I was a fool. She never told me why, and I couldn't make it out no way.

I set down one time back in the woods, and had a long think about it. I says to myself, if a body can get anything they pray for why don't Deacon Winn get back the money he lost on pork? Why can't the widow get back her silver snuff-box that was stole? Why can't Miss Watson fat up? No, says I to myself, there ain't nothing in it.

And if everybody who agreed with Huck Finn were to say "Amen" together, it would be heard around the world. We have prayed for health, and sickness has come; we have prayed for loved ones to get well, and they have died; we have prayed for material blessings, but they never came. Yes, we have prayed and it is as Huck Finn said, "Nothing come of it." So what is the answer?

In the fourth chapter of the Epistle of James, we read these words: "Ye ask, and receive not, because ye ask amiss. . . ." In that same chapter James tells us: "Submit yourselves therefore to God. . . ." On further he says, "Draw nigh to God, and he will draw nigh to you. . . ." Also, James says, "Humble yourselves in the sight of the Lord, and he shall lift you up."

The beginning of prayer is a right relationship with God; without that beginning we merely speak words and call them prayers. Recently a friend of mine gave me a beautiful electric lamp for my desk. Carefully and lovingly he made it for me and it is a thing of beauty. But suppose I take it home, turn the switch, and no light comes. I might conclude that all electric lamps are a fake. The trouble may be in the lamp. On the other hand, it may be that I failed to connect it to the source of power. The world

19

is filled with electricity, but until I connect my lamp to it, it will not burn.

So with prayer. I may use the most beautiful words and phrases, but until I am connected with the great Source of power, my prayers are just meaningless words. Jesus said some people ". . . think that they shall be heard for their much speaking. Be not ye therefore like unto them: for your Father knoweth what things ye have need of before ye ask him. After this manner therefore pray ye: Our Father which art in heaven, Hallowed be thy name" (Matt. 6:7–9). That is, before you consider the results of prayer, get connected with the Source.

Recently I spent five days in Florida conducting revival services. During the afternoons I would go out on the beach and watch the water. While there I thought of a woman that one of our great preachers tells about. She was sick and went to Florida to recuperate. Each day she would go out on the beach alone and there, in the midst of nature, she practiced deliberately turning her mind toward God.

One day she became acutely conscious of the deep silence of nature. The quietness was such that she could feel her heart beating. She began to notice the steady undeviating rhythm of her heart.

As she felt her heart beating, she turned her eyes and looked through the beach grass near her. She noticed how clean it had been washed by the tides. Also, she noticed that the grass moved slowly and gracefully to and fro with the gentle breeze. As she watched she became conscious that the grass, too, had a rhythm—the same rhythm as her heartbeat.

Then her eyes lifted to the sea and she watched the waves rise and fall and roll up on the clean sand. She suddenly became aware that it, too, had a rhythm, a rhythm like the waving of the grass and the beating of her heart. She began to realize that there is one fundamental harmony throughout the universe. She realized she was in tune with nature and she realized that God is the great Creator and, thus, she was in tune with Him. She said, "Now I know there is a power by which life can be recreated—one must be attuned to that power."

And there we see the beginning of prayer: the becoming attuned or connected with God, the Source of all strength and power. No need to turn on the switch, seeking the blessings of prayer, until first our lives become properly connected with God. That is why so many fail to get what they ask in prayer.

We must ask with faith. We remember how two blind men came to Jesus asking to be healed. To them Jesus said, "Believe ye that I am able to do this?" And they replied, "Yea, Lord." Then He touched their eyes and said, "According to your faith be it unto you" (Matt. 9:28, 29).

James M. Barrie wrote: "The reason birds can fly and we can't is simply that they have perfect faith, for to have faith is to have wings." That is, if we have the faith, we will somehow get the means to carry out that faith. The Wright brothers did have faith that men could fly and they developed the wings. When we ask God and when we ask with faith, immediately we rid our minds of our destructive failure thoughts and we begin to develop a marvelous confidence—a threefold confidence.

(1) We develop confidence in ourselves. A man who has lost his nerve is a pitiful creature. He shrinks from every task and he turns away from every opportunity. But when he believes in himself, he develops power and strength he did not know he had.

But on the other hand, we must remind ourselves that confidence in ourselves is not enough. It is good as far as it goes but it doesn't go far enough. We like to quote William E. Henley's poem, "Invictus," in which he talks about his "unconquerable soul," how under adverse circumstances he has not "winced or cried aloud" and how triumphantly he says, "I am the master of my fate, I am the captain of my soul." But in the end Henley committed suicide. He made a good try, but self-confidence was not enough.

(2) Also, when we believe, we develop faith in our friends. "No man liveth unto himself"—we need the support of each other. Why do men and women marry? It isn't just the physical relationship. Human beings have needs deeper than physical needs and true faith leads us to believe in the goodness and reliability of other people, and to draw strength from our friendships. But we have needs that human resources cannot supply. And so:

(3) True faith not only leads us to self-confidence and confidence in other people, it also leads us to have confidence in God. The Bible says, "But without faith it is impossible to please him: for he that cometh to God must believe that he is, and that he is a rewarder of them that diligently seek him" (Heb. 11:6). So for the person of faith, the philosophy of life, "Try asking God," has great meaning.

The best definition of prayer I know of is given in the Westminster Shorter Catechism—"Prayer is an offering up of our desires unto God for things agreeable to His will." That puts the center of prayer where it belongs—not on the things we ask for, but rather upon God and His will. But it also allows for the human side of prayer, that is, "our desires." We come to trust God's ability, His purposes, and His judgments and whatever His answer to our prayer may be, that is the answer we want.

Thus the Christian not only asks God, but to his asking he adds, "in Christ's name." To ask in Christ's name is to ask in the spirit of Christ. It means to pray the prayer that Christ would pray, if He were in our place. It means that we want to know the mind of God and the spirit of God, even as Christ knew it. And it means that our lives are committed to the will and the ways of God, even as Christ's life was so committed. The true end of prayer is not getting from God, but giving ourselves to God.

3

GOD IS A BIG GOD

The trouble with a lot of people is: their God is too small. St. Paul said, ". . . My God shall supply all your need . . ." (Phil. 4:19). In that statement he reveals that his God is a big God. But when you say, "My God," what do you mean?

I know of a man in New York who died recently at the age of seventy. As a young man of twenty, he married and opened a little shop on a side street. He and his wife lived in a tiny apartment on the East side. Six mornings a week he would get up, eat his breakfast, walk to the subway station and ride to his work. All day long he spent in his shop. Because he never had another clerk, he carried his lunch from home and ate on the job.

At closing time he would catch the subway back, eat his supper and soon go to bed. He was never a strong man so he rested in bed every Sunday. For fifty years that was his routine and then he died. When that man said "My city," he meant a tiny apartment, a subway train, and a shop on a side street. He never saw the Metropolitan Museum, or rode to the top of the Empire State Building, or mingled with the crowds on Fifth Avenue. "My city" was for him a very limited experience.

When you say "My God," what do you mean? For St. Paul, "My God" meant one great enough to cover his entire life—". . . shall supply all your need," he said. Unless your God is that big, then He is too small. As far as your individual life is concerned, I think God's size can be summed up in three statements:

(1) *God never will let you down*—". . . shall supply all your need." The psalmist had a God that big: "The LORD is my shepherd, I shall not want." That means nothing can happen to you that God is not able to handle. Observe those who came to Christ in need. Not one person could ever say, "Christ let me down." On the other hand, one after another could say, "Christ lifted me up."

As I turn through my Bible, I see on every page some word in regard to the providence of God. For example, the writer of Psalm 37 observed: "I have been young, and now am old; yet have I not seen the righteous forsaken, nor his seed begging bread." Come to think about it, I never have either. Many have I seen begging. Rarely a day passes that someone does not come to me, but when you go into the full story, you will find much that is unrighteous. I don't think we ought to be righteous just because it is good insurance; nevertheless, the fact remains.

When "My God" becomes bigger than my needs, it means the dread and fear of my life is taken away. That doesn't mean that no trouble will ever come our way. It does mean that God will supply the strength and resources we need to face that trouble. God will never let you down!

25

When you find a person who feels God has let him down, look closely and you will see that the fact is, the person let God down. I speak often to people about tithing because I believe that is one of the finest ways to prove our faith in God. He said, "Bring ye all the tithes into the storehouse . . . and prove me now herewith, saith the LORD of hosts, if I will not open you the windows of heaven, and pour you out a blessing, that there shall not be room enough to receive it" (Mal. 3:10).

But a lot of people don't believe God can keep that promise. Their God is not even as big as ten percent of their income. How big is your God? Big enough to supply all your needs? Or must you worry all the joy out of living today because of what might happen tomorrow?

How big is your God? He is big enough to meet all your needs. He never lets you down.

(2) But also *God never lets you off.* When He created this universe, He made the laws by which it operates. It has been a long time since the beginning, but the earth still revolves around the sun and the law of gravitation has not yet been repealed.

Likewise, God forged into this world the principles of life— love is better than hate, righteousness is better than sin, goodness is better than evil. But as we go along, we decide we don't want to be bound by the laws of God. So, instead of living up to God, we reduce God to the level of our living. We end up with a God too little to be the Lord of our lives.

Dr. J. B. Phillips speaks of the "Grand Old Man" idea of God. A child in Sunday school was asked to write down his idea of God. He wrote: "God is a very old gentleman living in heaven." Children read the Bible, which tells about God in the long, long ago. Because He lived so long ago, of course He must be a tottering old person by now!

There was a period in my life when I thought my own father was the oldest man in the world. Believing him to be old, it was easy for me to believe he was also old-fashioned. I thought he didn't really understand modern life. He grew up in the horse and buggy days and the automobile age was far beyond him, to say nothing of the plane. So as a cocky young man in my teens, I decided I knew more than he did, and didn't need to pay much attention to his counsel and guidance. You know, our two most interesting ages are six and eighteen. At six we know all the questions and at eighteen we know all the answers. Nearly all children have a period of life when they decide they have outgrown their parents.

We reach that same point with God. We know we should treat the "Grand Old Man" with reverence and respect, but we don't need to be bound by His old-fashioned ideas about life. After all, life is so complicated today that one who lived in Abraham's day could not be expected to understand it. Some psychologists gave a test to a group of teen-agers. The psychologist would ask a question and the youth was to reply without hesitation. One of the questions was, "Do you think God understands radar?" In nearly every case the answer was "No."

So when you decide you have outgrown an old-fashioned God, most of the moral conflict is eliminated. Instead of bothering about His will and His commands, we push Him aside and make our own laws and choose our own paths. In reference to God the Father, many people are lifetime teen-agers. Their God is not big enough to control their lives so they cast Him aside.

But remember, Jesus said that God is a Father. He never said God is an indulgent grandfather. A true father is one who keeps control over his children as long as they are children. The child may disobey, but the true father is compelled to punish that dis-

27

obedience. God is a true Father—we are His children and God never lets us off.

I was saying that (1) God never lets us down, (2) He never lets us off. Now I must say one thing more: (3) *God never lets us go.*

Once there was a boy who again and again broke the laws of the land and would end up in jail. His father would go down to pay his fine and get him free. Finally it cost the father about all that he had and also his heart was almost broken. A friend said to the father, "If that were my boy, I would let him go." He replied, "If he were your boy, I would too, but he is my boy and I can't let him go." Well, God is your Father and, no matter what happens, He is ever seeking to bring you back unto Himself.

There is an old book entitled *The Bishop of Cotton Town.* In that book is a man who lived a wicked life, caring only for his little daughter. He loved that little girl dearly. One day she died. The old preacher in that little mill town, affectionately called "the Bishop," came to see him. He said, "Jim, sometimes men repent when God smiles. They see the beauty of the flowers and hear the song of the birds. Sometimes men repent when God calls. They hear His voice through a sermon or in some other way. But Jim, sometimes men don't repent until God strikes them a blow in the face with His fist."

That is a good story but I cannot accept the theology of it. I do not believe God takes little children in order to punish parents or to force them to repent. God has a better way than that.

The true picture of God is the one Jesus gave us in the story of the Prodigal Son. When that boy wanted to leave home and get away from the authority of his father, he was free to go. As life went by for him, that boy had some blows in the face too, but his father didn't strike them. Life itself can be mighty cruel and hard and disappointing.

Neither did the father go after his boy and force him to return. Instead, the father maintained the home and one day that boy became hungry. Then he remembered his father and he came back. The father was there, with the door open, abundantly able to satisfy those hungers.

We sometimes talk about the "free will" God has given us, as if He has completely cut us loose from Himself. We are not so free. We do not have free will when it comes to eating or not eating. Our very hunger demands that we eat. And God built into us certain other hungers. It is possible to live away from God and never hunger for material things. But there comes a time when those material things do not satisfy. We have deeper soul hungers and those hungers are cords by which God has bound our soul.

God is patient and He can wait. But while He waits, the hungers of our soul keep us dissatisfied. We seek this and that, and rush hither and yon, but nothing we find in life supplies our deepest needs. Finally we turn to Him who said, "I am the bread of life: he that cometh to me shall never hunger . . ." (John 6:35). Yes, God never lets you go.

4

LEARNING GOD'S WILL

Someone has put the deepest question of mankind into just two little short words—"Why I?" In one form or another, that question has been in the minds of all of us. "Why I?" Until you ask and find the answer to that question, life can never mean its most to you.

"Why I?" I suppose there are some who never ask that question. Like pigs, they go wandering along through life with no goals or purposes, swallowing up whatever they can find that appeals to their appetites. That is the animal way of life. The higher human life searches for reasons to live. "Why I?" No more serious and important question can occupy your mind, and your real success in life is largely dependent upon your finding the answer to it.

We remember how Jesus said, ". . . I have finished the work which thou gavest me to do" (John 17:4). That statement reveals that God had a definite plan for Jesus' life, that He could and did know what that plan was, and that it was possible for Him to accomplish it. That was true for Christ; it is also true for each one of us. No one of us is here by accident nor by chance. God has a plan for your life—of that you can be sure.

However, God gave to each person power of choice and freedom of will. We remember how our Lord prayed, ". . . nevertheless not my will, but thine be done" (Luke 22:42). That prayer teaches two very important truths: first, one might have a will for his own life that is contrary to God's will for him. Second, it is possible to follow your own will and turn your back on God's will for you. Were those two facts not true, then Christ's prayer would have been mockery.

Each of us faces that same choice. There is a story about a very wise man who always gave the right answer to every question. One day a boy sought to trap him. He held a live bird in his hand and said, "Mr. Wise Man, is this bird in my hands alive or is it dead?" If the wise man said it was dead, he would open his hand and let the little bird fly away. If the wise man said it was alive, he would give his hands a quick squeeze and open them to show the dead bird.

Strangely, the wise man did not look at the boy's hands at all. Instead, he looked full into the boy's eyes and quietly said, "My son, it is whatever you wish it to be." So it is with each of us. The life we live is the one we wish to live—God's way or some other way. The choice is in our own hands.

But even when through faith in God we pray, "Thy will be done," we have not answered the question, "Why I?" What is His will for my own personal life? Many people have come to

31

me asking that question. Some are so confused that they wonder if God's will for them can be known.

The Bible says, "In all thy ways acknowledge him, and he
shall direct thy paths" (Prov. 3:6). How does God make known
His will to us?

John Oxenham has written in *Bees in Amber* (American Tract
Society, 1913):

> Not for one single day
> Can I discern my way,
>   But this I surely know,—
> Who gives the day,
> Will show the way,
>   So I securely go.

But, some insist, I have not seen the way and I am confused.

To begin with, God did much in showing us the way when He
made us. We are born with certain talents and abilities and God
plans for us to do what we can do. Also, we can know God's will
for us by considering our opportunities. We can be sure that God
provides the opportunity for the carrying out of His purposes.

Just a few days ago one of my church members, a lovely young
lady, was in my office saying, "I'm fed up with living. There is
nothing for me in life." I said to her, "It is God's will for you to
sing in the choir of this church." She asked, "How do you know
that?" "Because," I replied, "you have the talent to sing and the
choir needs you." Ability and opportunity, when those two come
together, whether it be in a small obscure way or in some more
prominent way, mark a clear indication of the will of God.

Second, often God makes known His will to us through the
direct workings of providence. Look at the life of Dr. Albert
Schweitzer, considered by many one of the great Christians of

all time. He was trying to settle on his life's work. He had so many abilities—for music, for medicine, for teaching—and today he is a master in each of those fields. There were uncounted opportunities for him. What should he do? What was God's plan for him?

One day he was cleaning out his desk. Among the papers there was a little magazine of the Paris Missionary Society. It was addressed to a neighbor but by mistake had been put in his mailbox. He glanced through it and noticed an article entitled, "The Needs of the Congo Mission." He read the article and when he finished, Dr. Schweitzer said, "My search was over." To the Congo he went and there he has lived one of the greatest lives any of us can imagine.

Let me ask you, was it just an accident that the postman put that little magazine in the wrong mailbox? Was it mere chance that it lay there for days unnoticed until just that moment when Dr. Schweitzer's mind was open to receive direction? No, we believe the hand of God was moving upon the life of that man. It is as the hymn-writer said, "God moves in a mysterious way."

There is something else to be seen in that experience. Dr. Schweitzer might have said, "I have too much to bury it in the faraway Congo." But he didn't say that. He was willing to lose himself in God's plan and it was as Jesus said it would be, ". . . he that loseth his life for my sake shall find it."

How can I know God's will for my life? I have suggested two ways; through a consideration of our own talents and opportunities; and through some special revelation of God. There are still other ways to know His will.

We may use our own best judgment. In the play *Green Pastures*, one says, "I guess de Lord means us to figure out a few things for ourselves." A man once said, "I prayed for advice but got no answer to my prayer, so I just used my common sense." But who gave that man his common sense?

The other day a man came in to see me, a man so confused he was sick. He said, "If somebody doesn't tell me what to do, I will go crazy." I suggested I could not tell him the answers until I knew the questions and thus I urged him to lay before me the entire situation. I listened quietly as he told me the story. Finally, he finished. I asked a few questions to clear some points I did not quite understand.

Then I told the man I wanted to think a few minutes before I told him the answer. Since he had known the story much longer than I had and had been thinking about it, I suggested that he give me the benefit of his own ideas as to what he should do. He hesitated a moment and then he said, "Well, this is what I have thought would be the best," and he outlined a marvelous solution. I said, "That seems to me a fine answer and the answer to your questions." The man got up, fervently thanked me and said I was the most sensible person he had ever talked to. He left a satisfied and calm man.

I didn't do anything for the man, except to encourage him to use his own mind. He had the ability all the time to find the answers but he had let fear and panic overrule his reason.

But I must mention a danger here. Sometimes we let the voice of inclination overrule our best judgment. Instead of thinking and reasoning, we are controlled by our passions or our selfish desires. We must be careful to include God in our thinking.

A dear lady whose husband had recently died was telling me that he did not leave a written will. But confidently she was going right ahead and making the decisions without hesitation. She told me, "I lived with him for forty years. I knew him so well that I know exactly what he would have done." Even though he did not write it, she knew her husband's will. How did she know

34

it? Through companionship with him day by day and year by year.

So it is with the will of God. As we live close to Him, read the Bible He inspired, talk with Him through prayer, worship Him with others in the services of the church, work with Him in the bringing of His Kingdom on earth, we do come to know Him and to love Him. In knowing God, we know His will. In loving God, we want to do His will. God directs our paths through friendship and companionship with us.

5

PRAYER BRINGS LIFE'S GREATEST HAPPINESS

Without doubt Jesus was the most joyful person who has ever lived. What was the reason for His joy? Dante summed it up when he said, "In His will is our peace." Jesus was totally dedicated to the will of God and that is the only pathway to true happiness in any life. I underscore the word *only*.

When we decide as Christ did, ". . . nevertheless not my will, but thine, be done" (Luke 22:42), it brings happy peace into our lives. That is true, for one reason, because it takes away from us the fear of getting lost in life. Some time ago I was in another city and a friend offered to bring me home in his little two-seater airplane. On the way we suddenly realized we were off course and were lost. We could see no landmarks to guide us, the ground below was rough, and there was no place to land. There was the fear of running out of fuel. There was no radio in the plane to check our course. For a time, life for us was a very uncomfortable experience.

On the other hand, not long ago I was flying in one of our big commercial airliners. We were in weather so cloudy that even the wing tips were invisible. I was up front talking with one of the pilots. I asked, "How do you know you are on the right track?" He told me to listen in over his earphones. I could distinctly hear the radio beam. Even though the pilot could not see thirty feet ahead, that invisible beam guided him straight to his field. He had no fear of getting lost.

It is fascinating to study the migration of birds. Take, for example, the Pacific Golden Plover. Those birds are hatched in the northlands of Alaska and Siberia. Before the young ones are old enough to fly great distances, the old birds desert them and fly far away to the Hawaiian Islands. The young birds are left behind to grow strong enough to follow their parents.

One day these birds rise into the sky and set their course out over the Pacific. They have never made that journey before and they must cross two thousand miles of ocean, with no marks to guide them. During this trip they have not even one opportunity to stop for rest or food and frequently they encounter high winds and storms. Yet unerringly they fly straight to those tiny specks in the Pacific, the Hawaiian Islands.

How do you explain the flight of these birds? Surely God has provided them something akin to our radio beams, something they can follow without getting lost. And I firmly believe God has made the same provisions for mankind. When our lives are in harmony with His will, even though we cannot see the way ahead, we have an instinctive sense of the right direction and, with courage and confidence, we move steadily ahead through life, without any fear of getting lost, knowing that through the storms and uncertainties, we shall come to the right place at last. That is a wonderful assurance to possess. "In all thy ways acknowledge him, and he shall direct thy paths" (Prov. 3:6).

This relieves us of the burden of the responsibility of tomorrow. If you will study your fears and worries, you will see that most of them are concerned, not with the failures and mistakes of yesterday, because in most cases you can overcome those. Neither are most of your fears and worries about things of this very moment, because you know you can make it through this day. But when you turn your face toward the dim unknown of tomorrow, you are not sure what lies in your path and as you wonder, often you worry and become afraid.

But when God asks us to follow His will, at the same time He is saying, "I will accept the responsibility for whatever happens." After Jesus had said on the cross, "It is finished," He then said, "Father, into thy hands I commend my spirit" (Luke 23:46). It was a cry of faith. He had done His best, He had given His all. Now He was willing to leave the results in God's hands.

Because we have faith in God, we can say with the hymnwriter, "Keep thou my feet: I do not ask to see the distant scene; one step enough for me." God usually does not make known His will to us for years ahead. Instead, He shows us one step at a time and as we take that step, we know it leads us that much closer to the very best possible life there is for each of us. What that life will turn out to be is not our responsibility—it is God's, and thus we need have no fear.

I am now thinking of some of the great tragedies many have been forced to face—the untimely death of a loved one, some physical deformity, a bitter disappointment which seems impossible to correct, and many others.

My answer is that the completion and fulfillment of God's will is not limited to this life here on earth. He plans in terms of eternity and though it may seem God is defeated, let us reserve our judgment until the complete story is written.

Another way that God's will brings us peace is by eliminating the conflicts within our lives. Instead of squandering our energies with countless decisions, wondering whether to do this or to do that, we can settle it with one great decision: "I shall do the will of God." That brings into our lives a singleness of purpose and thereby brings us peace and strength. We remember how St. Paul said, "This one thing I do." When we reach that point, most of the problems of life are solved. Accepting the will of God gives us the power of a great purpose.

Self-dedication to the will of God eliminates another type of conflict—the one between right and wrong. A man was in to see me some time ago about a wrong in his life. He wanted to do right, but he also wanted to do wrong, and in the resulting conflict he had become miserably unhappy. Truly, "In His will is our peace." That is true, for one reason, because when we follow God's will we have the approval of a good conscience.

I know that conscience is something hard to explain and, whatever it is, it must be trained and developed. Some people have done very evil things, yet they were following what they thought were the dictates of their conscience. But after the psychologists have said all they can in explaining the human conscience, and some of them even explain it completely away, still we recognize a voice within saying, "This is right; that is wrong."

We argue with ourselves and say, "Everybody else is doing it." But if inside we feel we have done wrong, we cannot be completely at peace until we have made it right. Huckleberry Finn was right when he said, "Conscience takes up more room than all the rest of a fellow's insides." When we do what God wants us to do, it makes us feel mighty good inside.

I now cherish many of the stories my father told me of his own life. One that I have thought about a great deal is something that I think bothered him all his life. I remember the sadness in his voice as he told it. When he was a boy, living up in the North Georgia mountains of White County, life was simple and they did not have many things.

One thing he especially wanted as a boy was a barlow knife. I really don't know what a barlow knife is but I think it is a simple pocket knife. Anyway, he wanted one more than almost anything else. One day his father was going to Gainesville and he told him to clean off a certain creek bank while he was away. For doing that job, he would bring him the barlow knife he so badly wanted.

Eagerly my father set out to do the work in happy anticipation of his father's return and the receiving of his blessed reward. The weather was hot and when he got down to the creek, the water was so inviting that he decided to take a short swim. As he played in the water, the time swiftly passed but, then, there was no special hurry. It took a long time for a wagon to go from Loudsville to Gainesville and back. He could easily get the work finished tomorrow. The next day, as he started his work, he happened to see some little fish jumping in the creek. It would do no harm to catch a few, so he dug some bait and the fish were biting. Again the hours sped by until the chance to get his job done was gone.

That night his father would be coming home. Faithful to his promise he would have that prized barlow knife. But that boy was now very unhappy. He would have to face his father and he would have to say, "I didn't do the job. I didn't earn the knife."

It is easy to think of our Lord. He had many temptations to turn aside, to waste His time and His life. In faithfully following His Father's will, sometimes the going was hard. But one day, the Bible says, He "lifted up his eyes to heaven, and said . . . I have finished the work which thou gavest me to do" (John 17:1, 4). As He hung on the cross, again He said, "It is finished" (John 19:30).

God has given us certain tasks in life. And I know of no greater happiness one can experience than to know he can face God saying, "I've done my best."

6

PRAYER AND PEACE
OF MIND

Listen to the melody of these words: "Thou wilt keep him in perfect peace, whose mind is stayed on thee: because he trusteth in thee" (Isa. 26:3). "Perfect peace"—is there any possession of life more desirable than that?

Many nights I drive a hundred or so miles to get home after some speaking engagement. Before I go to bed, I like to go by our children's rooms and look at their faces. They are sound asleep, perfectly relaxed, completely at peace. I wonder why the people I've seen today are not like that. Once we did have that peace but as we grow older our lives become more complicated.

We think of the living we have to make, the debts we owe, of what will happen to us in our old age. We worry about the world situation, we crossed up with other people, we think about the wrongs we have committed, we are afraid of our health. Gradually the peace of our minds is drained away and gone. "Whose mind is stayed on thee," said the prophet, is the way to perfect peace.

First, we need to learn to empty our minds. It is impossible to be at peace as long as we hold certain things in our minds. When we come in at night we wash our hands, sending down the drain the dirt we have picked up during the day. Wouldn't it be wonderful if we could wash our minds as we wash our hands?

After Rabbi Liebman wrote his book, *Peace of Mind,* he was swamped with people seeking that peace. His mail was heavy, his telephone rang constantly, people came to his study all day and even to his home at night. He was a kindhearted young man of only thirty-eight years. He tried to help every person and he died in three years, at forty-one. He just couldn't stand the burden. But before he died he said, "I am appalled at the multitudes of people who have never learned to empty their minds."

I know of a man who habitually brought his problems home with him at night. He talked about his troubles at the dinner table, brooded over them during the evening hours, took them to bed to keep him company during his troubled sleep. One night, as he turned off the pavement to the steps of his home, he hit upon a plan. "Tonight," he said, "I am leaving all my worries here on the steps. I'll pick them up again in the morning."

To do a thing like that requires mental discipline, but it can be done. That night he enjoyed his dinner, he found his family so much better companions; he slept better. But the best part, he explained, was that the next morning when he picked up his troubles as he walked down the steps, he found they were not nearly so heavy, and some of them were even gone entirely.

Instead of on the doorstep, there are some worries we need to learn to leave with God. Study carefully these words:

What a Friend we have in Jesus,
All our sins and griefs to bear!
What a privilege to carry
Everything to God in prayer!
O what peace we often forfeit,
O what needless pain we bear,
All because we do not carry
Everything to God in prayer!

If there is one message people need today, it is the message of the forgiveness of sins. We do not need to be told of our sins; we already know about them. A woman phoned me to say she was sixty-four years old, sick, and soon to die. Before she died she wanted something settled. She took ten dollars that didn't belong to her when she was twenty. Imagine carrying the burden of a guilt for forty-three years for only ten dollars! I told her about Him who said, "Neither do I condemn thee: go, and sin no more" (John 8:11). I wish every person knew about Him.

"Thou wilt keep him in perfect peace, whose mind is stayed on thee. . . ." We concentrate on our problems instead of our powers, on our fears instead of our faith, on our sins instead of our Savior, on our troubles instead of our triumphs.

The sales of a certain company were lagging badly, so the sales manager called his men in. He asked each man the trouble and they all spoke with feeling of the difficulties they were encountering and the reasons why it was hard to make sales. The manager put before them a large piece of white cardboard. He asked each man what he saw and each replied that he saw a piece of white cardboard.

The manager took a pencil and put a black dot in the center of the board and then asked each what he saw. Each replied that he saw a black dot. "That is your trouble," he explained.

"The moment one black spot appears you fix your attention on that and fail to see all the clean white space. So in your work, you concentrate on a few difficulties and fail to see all the possibilities."

We do the same thing in life. Most of life for each of us is happy and good. Yet some black spots are certain to appear from time to time. No life can be completely free of sorrows, disappointments, and failures. But to keep our minds stayed on those things will take away from us all the joy of living. The Bible says, "For as he thinketh in his heart, so is he . . ." (Prov. 23:7). What you think about is the most important factor in determining what your life will be.

A lady came to tell me of her worries and especially how they crowded in upon her after she had turned off the light and gone to bed. She would toss and turn until sheer exhaustion put her to sleep. In the morning she would wake up tired and nervous. She was completely missing the marvels of truly restful sleep.

I asked what she really enjoyed most and she told me of her flowers. She liked to grow them and especially to arrange them. She had won prizes at flower shows for her arrangements. She liked roses best. I suggested that at night, after getting into bed, she picture in her mind a table with two dozen beautiful roses on it, half deep red and half snow white. I suggested that in the center of the table she imagine a vase and then mentally begin picking up the roses one by one and arranging them. We talked of various ways they could be arranged—the reds on one side and the whites on the other, mixed with each other, etc.

That is a simple little idea but it worked a miracle for that lady. And it is in line with the advice of St. Paul, "Whatsoever things are lovely . . . think on these things" (Phil. 4:8). Instead of roses, some would rather think of some particular person whom they admire. Just for more relaxation, I personally can

45

lose myself in a game of mental golf. But I want to say something more important about this.

There is one song I would especially like to teach to every person. It isn't great music but it is in accord with the religious principles of the Bible. The words of the first verse are:

> When upon life's billows you are tempest-tossed,
> When you are discouraged, thinking all is lost,
> Count your many blessings, name them one by one,
> And it will surprise you what the Lord hath done.

When we are physically upset, we go to the doctor, have his prescription filled and faithfully take the medicine. But when we are mentally upset we often refuse to do some simple things that will really do us good. That little song, for instance. Many dismiss it as being silly but I urge you to try exactly what it says. When "thinking all is lost," take pencil and paper and begin to list your blessings one by one. Soon you will fill a page and it will work a marvelous change in your thinking. Try it.

But there is something better with more abiding results. The Bible says, "Thou wilt keep him in perfect peace, whose mind is stayed on thee." Having our minds stayed on God is the most effective psychiatry we can experience.

During the war many boys could not stand the strain of the battlefield. They would be sent back to some hospital with what they called "battle fatigue." After rest, most of them would be all right but at times some of these soldiers were mentally disturbed to the point of violence. One day a young intern was walking through a large ward containing many of these cases.

Suddenly a man jumped out of bed, grabbed him around the throat and said, "You are my enemy. You are trying to kill me so I am going to kill you." The intern knew he couldn't handle that man. He was twice as strong as the doctor normally and now he had the strength of a maniac. One twist of those hands and his neck would be broken.

Instead of fighting, the doctor completely relaxed, looked the man straight in the eye and quietly said, "The Lord is my shepherd; I shall not want." The man looked at him, his eyes began to focus. "Yea, though I walk through the valley of the shadow of death, I will fear no evil." A semblance of sanity began to come back into the man's face, his hands on the doctor's throat began to ease up.

With slow deliberation, the doctor repeated the Twenty-third Psalm. Finally he said, "Surely goodness and mercy shall follow me all the days of my life; and I will dwell in the house of the Lord forever." The soldier was relaxed. The doctor took him by the arm and said, "Come on now, let's go back to bed." And it is amazing how the troubles of life become docile before the one whose mind is stayed on God.

A very prominent businessman told me of how he learned all over again to pray, "Now I lay me down to sleep. . . ." He said he thought he had outgrown that prayer but now that he has learned it again, he considers it the most valuable possession of his life. "Whose mind is stayed on God"—that is the pathway to perfect peace.

7

THREE IMPERATIVES: FAITH, HOPE, LOVE

One of the finest verses in all the Bible is this one: "And now abideth faith, hope, love, these three; but the greatest of these is love" (1 Cor. 13:13). Underscore that word *abideth*. It is a strong and sturdy word.

Henry Francis Lyte was an old man, near the end of his life's journey. The doctors had told him he had only a few months to live. He was tired and ill. One day he sat down at his desk and picked up his Bible. It fell open to one of his favorite passages and he read: "Abide with us: for it is toward evening, and the day is far spent . . ." (Luke 24:29). He read and reread those words. Suddenly he was tired no longer. Words, thrilling words, began to fill his mind. He began writing:

Abide with me! fast falls the eventide;
The darkness deepens: Lord with me abide!
When other helpers fail, and comforts flee,
Help of the helpless, O abide with me!

He gained marvelous new strength in the realization that he possessed something that would abide.

Study the possessions people today are seeking and you will see that so many of these things are only temporary—clothes that will be out of style next year, cars that will wear out, treasures that "moth and rust doth corrupt." So often we are disappointed in these things after we possess them. The joy many things bring is overshadowed by the realization that soon it will be gone. Every material blessing we have will one day be lost, physical strength will one day become weakness, the years will steal away our beauty. The most brilliant career will soon come to an end. The most thunderous applause will die into silence. Even if you are perfectly satisfied with life today, you will not be satisfied tomorrow.

How much better to possess some things that will last. After a long lifetime of study and experience, one of the wisest and best men who ever lived named three things within our reach that will abide. They are: faith, hope, love. Not only will they last; they give marvelous character to the life which possesses them.

Consider *faith*. Without it we are not sure of ourselves. It is hard for us to make decisions. We are afraid to dare, to dream, to adventure. When Admiral Du Pont was explaining to Admiral Farragut the reasons why he failed to enter Charleston Harbor with his fleet of ironclads, Farragut listened until he was through and then said, "Du Pont, there is one reason more." "What is that?" Du Pont asked. Farragut's answer was, "You did

49

not believe you could do it." Without faith, any person's life is filled with dreary failures.

And failing to possess faith, we look at our fellow men with suspicion and cynicism. We miss the comfort and stimulation of real friendships. We think the world is against us. We lose our enthusiasm for living.

Losing faith, we lose our great ideals and purposes, and life takes on a weaker tone. Without faith, we become possessed with a "What's-the-use" attitude.

What is faith? There are many definitions but essentially it means two things: first, to continue to believe in certain truths, no matter what happens. Let me illustrate: A temptation comes to be dishonest. It is easy to think of the advantages to be gained, to say, "This one time won't matter." But one also believes in the principles of honesty and truth. Faith means taking hold of the right principles and being loyal to them.

Faithfulness is standing by what you believe, no matter what happens. One of the grandest statements St. Paul made was this one: "I have kept the faith." Life dealt with him harshly but through it all he held to his faith. When one turns aside from what he knows is the highest and best, he is not keeping faith.

Second, the other part of faith is illustrated when man faces up to life and knows that he is unable to get the best of it, he depends on a higher help. For me, faith means three things about God:

(1) God created this world. That means that at the very heart of things are the principles of God. For a time it may seem that evil will triumph but we remember how He said, "I am Alpha and Omega, the beginning and the ending . . ." (Rev. 1:8). God was the beginning, in the end God will win.

(2) Faith means God cares. There come times when one feels forgotten and deserted. I wrote to a boy who is now located thousands of miles away. He wrote back, "Your letter made me feel that I have not been forgotten." When one is forgotten, there is little inspiration for living.

(3) Faith means God is working with us and not just watching us from afar. This does not mean that everything that happens is His will. Many things happen that hinder His will but He continues to work; and in the end, God's will triumphs.

St. Paul says, "Now abideth faith. . . ." No matter what happens, faith will last.

There is something else that will abide. It is *hope*. "Now abideth faith, hope. . . ." Hope is a word big and strong, but we have so watered it down that to us it represents little more than wishful thinking. "I hope it won't rain tomorrow," we say. Or, "I hope you will have a good vacation," or, "I hope everything will turn out all right."

But hope is more than wishful thinking; it is a firm expectation based on certain fundamental truths and actions. Hope is never a substitute to clear thinking and hard work. On the contrary, hope leads one to think and to work. The foundation of hope is belief in God. The psalmist said ". . . hope thou in God. . . ." Read more of the sentence: "Why art thou cast down, O my soul? and why art thou disquieted in me? hope thou in God . . ." (Ps. 42:5).

A great Scottish preacher has well pointed out that the real profanity of man is not some swear words we use. Those words are more stupid than sinful. The most profane word we use, he said, is the word "hopeless." When you say a situation or a person is hopeless, you are slamming the door in the face of God.

When you become discouraged, when life looks utterly dark, when your plans have failed, then you can take one of three ways out. First, there is the way of the fool. He says, "This is hopeless, so I'll quit it." "I don't like this job; I'll get another one." "This thrill has let me down; I'll get a new one." "My marriage is no fun any longer; I'll break it up." "I can't face this situation; I'll run away from it." The fool is always quitting. He never holds to hope.

A second way to face the troubles of life is the cynic's way. It is a little better than the fool's way but not much better. He believes everything turns out badly. "This is just my luck," he says. "There is no joy in life for me, I'll just bear it as best I can." He never expects much and thus he is never very disappointed.

A third way to face life is the way of hope. Of course there will be disappointments and setbacks, but hope sees the sunshine coming behind the storm. God gave us ears with which to hear because there is music to be heard. The Christian believes that. Also, he believes God gave us eyes because there is beauty to be seen. Also, he believes God gave us the ability to hope because there is something finer and better ahead and if we keep going, we shall find it. Along with faith, real hope will never die.

"And now abideth faith, hope, love, these three . . ." the Bible says. *Love* is the third thing which is permanent and which will sustain a life, no mater what happens. The Bible goes on to say, "but the greatest of these is love" (1 Cor. 13:13). As great and important as faith and hope are, love is even greater.

So that there be no misunderstanding, before the great Apostle makes that statement, he analyzes love and shows us what it really is. His is the finest analysis of love in existence. It is contained in the thirteenth chapter of 1 Corinthians. Look carefully at real love and consider it well.

To begin with, Paul would have us know what love is not. It is not eloquent speaking and fancy language. Neither is love the ability to see with wisdom into the future nor is it the accumulation of much knowledge. Love is not faith that enables one to do big things. Love is not even the gifts we make or the service we render.

On the other hand, there are certain things love is. First, it is patience. The dictionary says patience is: "The suffering of affliction, pain, toil, calamity, provocation or other evil, with a calm unruffled temper; it is endurance without murmuring or fretfulness." "Love suffereth long . . ." Paul says. Love knows how to stand up to life and take it with a calm spirit.

Someone has named the three greatest personalities in the New Testament as Christ, Stephen, and Paul. Note the attitude of those three in the face of injustice and pain: "Father, forgive them . . ." said Christ. As Stephen was stoned he prayed, "Lord, lay not this sin to their charge." As Paul was about to be executed, he said, ". . . I pray God that it may not be laid to their charge." There is love, patient in suffering.

"Love suffereth long, and is kind. . . ." It is no accident that in analyzing love, St. Paul connects those two activities of love together. It is possible for one to suffer negatively. One can draw into a shell and suffer alone. But kindness is positive action. It does something constructive. Love doesn't just calmly suffer— it returns good even for evil.

There are other qualities of love. Love "envieth not." When something good happens to another person, love is glad. Love doesn't boast, "vaunteth not itself." The underlying cause of boasting is a desire to be superior and to dominate those around us. Envy, boastfulness—both are signs of an inferiority complex. Paul couples another quality of love with those two, "love . . . is not puffed up." We understand what he means by persons being "puffed up." Their feelings are hurt, they easily take offense, they pout. Or he may refer to one conceited and filled with false pride. Someone has written: "Are ye able to suffer without complain-

ing—To be misunderstood without explaining—Able to give
without receiving—To be ignored without any grieving—Able
to ask without commanding—To love despite misunderstanding—Able to turn to the Lord for guarding—Able to wait for
His rewarding?"

There are some more qualities of love. Note these five that
St. Paul puts together in one sweeping, magnificent sentence:
"Doth not behave itself unseemingly, seeketh not her own, is
not easily provoked, thinketh no evil; Rejoiceth not in iniquity,
but rejoiceth in the truth."

Then Paul concludes his God-inspired analysis of love with
four positive actions of love: "Beareth all things, believeth all
things, hopeth all things, endureth all things." Beareth—
believeth—hopeth—endureth. The order in which he lists these
is very important. The two extremes—beareth and endureth—
are similar qualities, but in between them and undergirding them
he puts: believeth—hopeth. Those two center words save and
redeem love from just bearing and just enduring.

Believeth and hopeth are words with a future. Love recognizes the reality of the pain, but beyond the pain love sees a victory and a triumph. Love is a creative force that can bring good
out of evil, even redemptive power out of a cross. In its final
analysis, love is greater than either faith or hope because it
includes both of those and adds a great deal more.

I stood the other day at George Washington Carver's grave.
I thought of him as a slave boy and also as the great man he
became. I wondered, if I had seen him as that slave boy, if I could
have visualized him as the man. Well, love looks at every unlikely
situation and sees its possibilities. "Love never faileth. . . ."

8

THE TIDE WILL COME IN

Recently I spent some weeks at Sea Island, Georgia, the most beautiful and inspiring place I know of anywhere. The homes, trees, and flowers there are as lovely as man working with God can make them.

But especially was I fascinated by the sea. I would go to sleep at night to the melody of the breakers coming in upon the shore. I would eat breakfast each morning on the porch looking out across the vastness of the water. Each day I would walk several miles down the beach. I would swim out into the deep and then ride the waves back in.

Sometimes I would become almost overwhelmed with how big the ocean is and how little I am. Looking at the ocean, one almost feels a sense of helplessness. We recall that Lord Byron once wrote:

Roll on, thou deep and dark blue ocean, roll!
Ten thousand fleets sweep over thee in vain;
Man marks the earth with ruin,—his control
Stops with the shore.

As you look at the ocean you realize: here is something bigger than any man, even bigger than all men.

Then you remember that the Bible says, "In his hand are the deep places of the earth . . . The sea is his and he made it" (Ps. 95:4, 5). There is One who is bigger than even the ocean, there is a God who is not helpless before it. There is a God who can and does control the sea. Realizing that, your faith is strengthened and you feel serene and unafraid.

As you live by the ocean for a time, there comes a better understanding of life because the two are so much alike. Life itself has a vastness that is beyond the reach of our sight. Just as we are told, "In his hand are the deep places of the earth . . ." also we can say with the psalmist, "I trusted in thee, O LORD . . . My times are in thy hand . . ." (Ps. 31:14, 15). We believe nothing can happen in our lives that God cannot handle. That gives us confidence and faith as we think of tomorrow.

There are many parallels between life and the ocean, but one especially impresses me—the coming and going of the tides. The tides go out and are low, the tides come in and are high. There is no power of earth that can prevent the low and high tides. So it is with an individual life—we experience times of low tide and of high tide and there is no way to stop those tides.

If we realize that we will experience low tides of our spirit, then our moments of depression and discouragement lose much of their terror. Even the true saints, those whose lives have been most completely in the hands of God, knew times when things seemed dark and when the shining of God's eternal light was very dim. There are times when we do not have a sense of the fullness of God's power or the realization of His presence. Then we say even as Christ said, "My God, my God, why hast thou forsaken me" (Matt. 27:46). What can we do when the tide of life is low?

The psalmist said, "Why art thou cast down, O my soul?" and we ask that same question.

We recall the marvelous Aldersgate experience of John Wesley, at which time he felt his heart "strangely warmed" and knew that his sins had been forgiven. It was a genuine Christian experience. But less than one year later Wesley wrote in his *Journal*, "I know that I am not a Christian. I know it because I do not feel that I love God and His Son Jesus Christ as my Saviour." There it is. There was the time when the power and love of God filled his life—but there also came the moment when the glory was gone.

Many times I have had phone calls from some frantic person saying, "I must see you today. I just cannot go on." But often circumstances would be such that I could not see the person that day. Several days later when I had time, I would telephone and the person would say, "I feel better now. I will be all right." What happened? The tide had come in.

Down at the lower end of Sea Island is a sandbar. At low tide it shuts off the island from the sea. It would block the progress of a boat. But at high tide the sandbar is covered and out of sight. One could ride a small boat across the bar and out into the deep waters. Just so there are times when our lives are blocked by some circumstance. Try as we may, we cannot go forward. But at other times those difficulties do not hold us back. The difference lies in whether the tide is low or high in our life. If the tide is low, there are times when all we can do is wait for the tide to come in.

Notice these three statements from the Bible—they seem contradictory: "For every man shall bear his own burden" (Gal. 6:5); "Bear ye one another's burdens . . ." (Gal. 6:2); "Cast thy burden upon the LORD . . ." (Ps. 55:22). But when you study the words which are translated "burden," you see they have different meanings. The "burdens" which we are to bear are our rightful obligations of life. The "burdens" of others which we are to bear are those extra burdens which are too heavy for one person, those unexpected troubles. But the "burdens" which we are to cast upon the Lord refer to those which are beyond human hands and help.

For example, when a person's house is carried away in a flood, neighbors rally around to help. But when a person's dearest loved one is carried away by death, though the handclasp of a friend helps, it does not heal. There are times when God is our only refuge and help. As the hymn-writer put it, "When other helpers fail, and comforts flee, Help of the helpless, O abide with me!"

When those burdens come that we cannot possibly bear, then we "wait for the tide." In his "The Ring and the Book," Browning uses a wonderful line: "I knew a necessary change in things." Our moments of defeat and sorrow are hard to bear but we do bear those moments because we are certain of the "necessary change in things." The tide may go out, but just as surely, it comes back.

Once some engineers were faced with the problem of lifting some very heavy parts of a bridge which crossed over a bay of the ocean. There were no cranes large enough to lift that load, so they lashed large pontoons under the bridge. Then they waited.

Slowly the tide came in with its tremendous power. Bit by bit the bridge was lifted. The tide represented not only the power of the ocean, but also of the moon and the sun and the other planets of the universe. And there is nothing too heavy for the power of the universe to lift. So it is with the burdens of life. At times we are helpless within our own power, but there is a power greater than man can imagine, the very power of the universe which will work on behalf of men. Learn to "wait for the tide."

The Bible teaches the principle of "waiting for the tide," again and again. For example, a low-tide experience is a time when we become discouraged. All persons are subject to both elevated and depressed moods. And when discouragement does come, and come it will, remember these words: "Wait on the LORD: be of good courage, and he shall strengthen thine heart: wait, I say, on the LORD" (Ps. 27:14). Or these words: "Why art thou cast down, O my soul? . . . hope thou in God . . ." (Ps. 41:11). Wait for the tide which God shall bring in.

Sometimes we get nervously overwrought. We want control, calmness, and peace but there seems nothing we can do. In such times we need to learn to "wait for the tide." To help in such low-tide times, remember these words from the Bible: "Rest in the LORD, and wait patiently for him . . ." (Ps. 37:7). That verse tells us to be still and rest; but when we are in a nervous, depressed state that is difficult. The psalmist knew that, so he said, "Rest in the LORD." Picture in your mind the greatness and goodness of God. Say to yourself, "My times are in His hands." And you gain serenity and quietness. Think of the mighty tides of the ocean and learn to "wait for the tide."

Sometimes the burdens of sorrow are so heavy we cannot bear them. But sorrow is a natural part of the experience of living. In the midst of this low tide of life, we need to learn to "wait for the tide." Listen to these words from the Bible: "For his anger endureth but a moment; in his favour is life: weeping may endure for a night, but joy cometh in the morning" (Ps. 30:5). Your agony is not permanent. Though a dark night seems to be settling down upon you, the morning will come. So you carry on through your sorrow, knowing it will bring you to the brightness of a new day.

I was in New York the other day and saw one of the giant ships of the sea coming in. It was beautiful and powerful and proud. But majestic as it was, that great ship had to wait for the tide before it could come in. The captain was anxious to make port. There were passengers on board who were in a hurry to land. But no matter—they must wait for the tide.

And there are times when we are anxious to make some port of victory, to accomplish some task; but also, there are times when we must "wait for the tide." But in the waiting, we are certain the tide will rise, and because of that certainty we have faith and hope.

9

YOUR UNSATISFIED DESIRES

Is there a more amazing statement in the entire Bible than this one? "Ask, and it shall be given you; seek, and ye shall find; knock, and it shall be opened unto you: For everyone that asketh receiveth; and he that seeketh findeth; and to him that knocketh it shall be opened" (Matt. 7:7, 8).

Amazing though it is, we know that statement is true. It is true because Jesus spoke it and He never spoke anything but the truth. We believe it. Why can't we actually practice it?

Do you know Hugh Price Hughes' story called "The City of Everywhere"? He arrived in that city one cold morning. As he got off the train, the station was like any other station with the crowds and redcaps, except that everybody was barefooted. They wore no shoes. He noticed the cab driver was barefooted. "Pardon me," he asked the driver, "I was just wondering why you don't wear shoes. Don't you believe in shoes?" "Sure we do," said the driver. "Why don't you wear them?" asked the man. The driver replied, "Ah, that's the question. Why don't we wear shoes? Why don't we?"

At the hotel it was the same. The clerk, bell boys, everybody was barefooted. In the coffee shop he noticed a nice-looking fellow at a table opposite him who also was barefooted. He said, "I notice you aren't wearing shoes. I wonder why? Don't you know about shoes?" The man replied, "Of course I know about shoes." "Then why don't you wear them?" "Ah, that's the question," said the man. "Why don't we? Why don't we?"

After breakfast he walked out on the street in the snow but every person he saw was barefooted. He asked another man about it and pointed out how shoes protect the feet from cold. The man said, "We know about shoes. See that building yonder? That is a shoe manufacturing plant. We are proud of that plant and every week we gather there to hear the man in charge tell about shoes and how wonderful they are." "Then why don't you wear shoes?" The man replied, "Ah, that's the question."

Dr. Robert E. Goodrich, Jr., tells this story in his book, *What's It All About*. Then he adds: "Don't we believe in prayer? Don't we know what it could mean to our lives? . . . Of course we do; we know about prayer. Then, why don't we pray? Ah, that's the question. Why don't we pray . . . Why don't we?"

Many answers as to why we don't pray are given, such as: our lives are crowded and hurried and we don't take the time. A man actually said to me, "I enjoyed the altar prayers in your church on Sunday night, but the time of my favorite television program has been changed. I had either to give up the prayer time or the program so I gave up the prayer."

Some would say we don't pray because we lack faith; or, because we don't know how to pray; or, because there are things in our lives which make us ashamed to face God. None of these are the real reasons. Why don't we pray?

We believe in prayer. Then why don't we pray? The real reason is, we have nothing to pray for. We have everything we want without praying. The supreme tragedy of most people is that they want so little and they are satisfied with almost nothing.

Dr. Charles M. Crowe in his book *Sermons from the Mount* says prayer is for the adventurous life. No call to adventure—no need for prayer. He tells about a certain man who had retired. Every morning he would get up and read the obituary column in the newspaper to see if his own name were there. If he wasn't listed among the dead, he would go back to bed for the remainder of the day.

A lot of people are satisfied just to be alive. They have no high dreams and lofty hopes, no great ambitions and burning desires. Someone took a survey and found that nine out of ten people have no definite plan in life. They just drift along and are content with whatever comes. Wanting nothing, they pray for nothing.

In contrast, listen to these words of Dean Alfange: "I do not choose to be a common man. It is my right to be uncommon— if I can. I seek opportunity—not security. I do not wish to be a kept citizen, humbled and dulled by having the state look after me. I want to take the calculated risk; to dream and to build, to fail and to succeed. I prefer the challenges of life to the guaranteed existence; the thrill of fulfillment to the stale calm of Utopia." There is a man who prays. He has a reason to pray.

Henry J. Kaiser is a man who prays. He says, "Your plan for work and happiness should be big, imaginative and daring. . . . The definite, faraway goal will supercharge your whole body and spirit; it will awaken your mind and creative imagination, and put meaning into your otherwise lowly, step-by-step everyday tasks." "The definite faraway goal"—not having that is why we don't pray.

For years we have been hearing that the chemical elements of the human body are worth only ninety-odd cents. But now it is known that the atoms in a human body have an energy potential of 11,400,000 kilowatt hours per pound, that is, worth $570,000,000. I weigh 150 pounds so that means I am worth $85,500,000,000. When you look at me, you are looking at one who is a billionaire 85 times. Why shouldn't I reach for the stars? Why should I be content with so little? Why shouldn't you reach out for something big?

Yet so many people get nothing because they want nothing. Jesus said, "Ask . . . seek . . . knock" (Matt. 7:7). But Jesus also said, ". . . your Father knoweth what things ye have need of, before ye ask him" (Matt. 6:8). Then why must we ask? We give our own children many things they need whether they ask or not—food, clothes, a bed to sleep in. But many things you can't give until they ask—an education, for example. The asking is not a condition of God's giving but rather a condition of our ability and willingness to receive.

Deep desire will lead you to: "Ask . . . seek . . . knock." In college my favorite subject was Greek. I worked hard at it and got to the stage where I could read Greek about as well as I could English. But through the years I have neglected my Greek and now all I use it for is to look up certain words to better understand their meanings.

These three "prayer words" in the original Greek are in the present tense and they call for continuing action. The better translation is "Keep on asking, keep on seeking, keep on knocking." Life is both alike and different from mountain climbing.

Alike in that the climber is constantly struggling higher; different in that in life we never reach the top. In life we never arrive because we never run out of heights to climb. The moment we give up the struggle of the climb, we begin to fall back and die.

Someone asked Raphael, "Which is your greatest painting?" He said, "My next one." That is the spirit that made him great.

Notice the order and meaning of these words: "Ask" is first. A child asks its father for something. It is really an admission of helplessness. The child cannot earn it or provide it for himself. The man on the corner who is blind asks for help. He is merely begging, he offers nothing in return. And before God there are many times we can only come asking. However, we are His children and that gives us the right to ask without shame.

"Seek" is the next word. That means asking plus effort. The boy who goes asking for a job is at the same time offering his service. Many of God's gifts come not in the form of pure gold, but in ore to be dug out of the earth. The gold is there, only awaiting our effort. That is as it should be. We don't want to go through life as mere beggars.

"Knock." Jesus told a story of a man who continued to knock on his neighbor's door at midnight until the man inside got up and answered his request (Luke 11:5–8). Knocking means asking plus effort plus persistence.

Read the life story of Florence Nightingale to see a real example of prayer. At the age of seventeen she felt called of God to be a nurse and she aspired to it. But blocking her path was the opposition of a neurotic mother, the prejudice against careers for women, and the antagonism of the medical profession. She wouldn't give up. She kept on asking, seeking, and knocking but it wasn't until she was thirty that her prayer was answered.

Jesus said, "Ask, and it shall be given you." That doesn't mean the exact thing you ask will be given. The promise is that something will be given. God may have something much better than you ask for. The faith to pray must include faith in God's love and His plan.

In Lloyd C. Douglas's novel, *The Big Fisherman*, a Roman officer prays for Peter's life. But Peter is condemned to die. The officer says, "I have prayed for you but it hasn't done any good." "I'm sure it has," says Peter. "I haven't been afraid."

10

SURRENDERING
YOUR DESIRES

You are doing right when you lay before God your plans and desires and ask His help. However, before God really opens the door He must hear you saying, ". . . nevertheless not my will, but thine, be done" (Luke 22:42). And I must warn you, that is a dangerous prayer to pray. Jesus prayed, "Thy kingdom come. Thy will be done in earth . . ." and God answered that prayer through a blood-soaked, humiliating, death-dealing cross.

The fact that prayer is dangerous never occurs to some. We think of prayer as being about the safest thing we can do—but it isn't. Do you remember singing the hymn: "I'll go where you want me to go, dear Lord, O'er mountain, or plain, or sea"? When we sing those words we usually think of the heroic life of some missionary. But be careful before you promise God you'll go where He wants you to go. He might not send you to Africa.

Instead, he might send you to apologize to and to forgive a certain person. Or He might send you to some obscure service in the church. Or He might send you to render an unpleasant service to some other person.

We sing lustily the hymn which says: "Take my silver and my gold; Not a mite would I withhold." You know, God has already reserved a tithe of our incomes but some of us refuse to recognize that. Some just flatly reject God's claim. And others try to outfigure God.

In so many ways we are not sincere when we pray, and that is why God does not hear us. But if you decide to be honest with God, then I must warn you to be careful what you pray for—you will surely get it. It takes great courage and faith to pray "nevertheless"—to relinquish our wills to God's will. But if we do really pray and mean that "nevertheless," then it brings marvelous peace and great power.

After Jesus' struggle in Gethsemane was over, a beautiful peace fell upon His spirit. Nothing could frighten or disturb Him after that. The soldiers came, He was tried, ridiculed, deserted, and crucified; but within His heart was calm peace. And really, isn't peace of mind and heart what we truly want in life? Isn't that our deepest prayer? Wouldn't we give up any possession for it? I don't know how God will answer your prayer but I do know that if you believe, He will answer it. Believe that God loves you, that He wants your life to be good and happy, that He has the power to supply your every need.

This doesn't mean that we are not to plan and to decide other things to pray for. God uses us for specific purposes and He wants us to receive certain of His gifts and blessings. But above all, He wants us to put Him first. It is as Jesus said, "But seek ye first the kingdom of God, and his righteousness; and all these things shall be added unto you" (Matt. 6:33).

It is the matter of the surrender of our wills to God's will that is hard for us. Most of the time God's will is not a known factor and thus it requires faith on our part. Starr Daily tells of a mother who came asking her minister to pray for her son who was sick. The minister asked, "If you knew it were God's will, would you be willing to let Billy go to heaven?"

It was a struggle for her but finally she said, "Yes, if I knew for sure it were God's will I'd be willing to release the boy." The minister prayed and later the child was healed. But it might have gone the other way. The important thing for us to know, however, is that God's will is always the best way for us. If we can believe that, our prayers will always be answered.

"And all things, whatsoever ye shall ask in prayer, believing, ye shall receive" (Matt. 21:22). That is a glorious promise and the key word in it is "believing." Oftentimes we wonder if God does hear our prayers and if, hearing, He has the power to answer or if He will answer.

Too often we are like the man who came to Christ seeking help for his sick son. He said, ". . . if thou canst do any thing, have compassion on us, and help us." Notice where he puts the "if." "If thou canst do any thing," he says. His "if" is in reference to Christ but gently the Lord corrects that man and replies, "If thou canst believe, all things are possible to him that believeth" (Mark 9:22, 23). The "if" is not with God, it is with the man.

The only limit to your prayer, says Christ, is the limit of your own belief. What is belief? It is mental visualization. It is seeing in your mind what you want accomplished in your life. Before a building is built, the architect draws the plans. First the building is put on a blueprint and any building that can be blueprinted can be actually built. I think it was Edison who said, "Science can create anything it can conceive of."

69

Believing is drawing a mental blueprint and, when you accomplish that, the word "impossible" is eliminated from your thinking. When you see it clearly in your mind, it may not yet be actual but you will know it is possible. To help in the process of believing, I suggest three preliminary steps:

(1) Write it down. You will find this difficult to do but keep working at it. Before an architect decides on the final drawings of a house, he makes many sketches and as he goes along he erases and redraws many lines.

(2) After you have what you really want written, read it over several times each day, making such additions and changes as you desire. When you have it clearly stated, then reduce what you have written to not more than fifty words.

(3) Consider your own resources and ask yourself what price you are willing to pay to have your prayer answered. Often it is that God has already answered our prayers. By that I mean, He has already given us the resources, and it only remains for us to apply those resources properly. But sometimes we don't really want our prayers answered because the price we must pay, we feel, is too high. God sometimes answers our prayers independently of us, but usually He answers through us.

God wants you to have a happy and successful life. Without your asking, He has given you marvelous resources—a mind to think with, hands to work with, friends to help and encourage, and a world of unlimited abundance. Even now He may be saying to you as Caleb said to the Children of Israel about the Promised Land, "Let us go up at once, and possess it; for we are well able to overcome it" (Num. 13:30).

In considering the matter of answered prayer, let us remember the words of Christ to the paralyzed man. He was praying to be well but Jesus asked him definitely: "Wilt thou be made whole?" (John 5:6). That is, do you really want your prayer answered? Then said Jesus, "Rise, take up thy bed, and walk." God had already answered that man's prayer but the man had not taken advantage of it.

Peter Marshall told of a woman who had been sick and who prayed to get well. But one day she seemed to hear God saying, "Is that what you really want?" As she pondered that question, she realized she had grown fond of her quiet life. There were no dishes to wash and no floors to sweep and none of the struggles of life to face. God clearly said to her, "As you take up your active life again, you will get well."

Then, when I really know what I want to pray for, and when I fully dedicate my own resources to helping answer my own prayer, I remember the words of Christ: "The things which are impossible with men are possible with God". (Luke 18:27). So, what resources I lack, I confidently ask God to supply.

However, now comes the supreme condition for receiving God's help. To see it clearly, let us look at our finest example. Many times our Lord prayed but the height of His prayers was reached that night in Gethsemane. The one purpose to which He was dedicated was the building of the Kingdom of God on earth. We know that as a lad of twelve years He was committed to that purpose: ". . . I must be about my Father's business," He said (Luke 2:49). We know that He studied and gave His all to that purpose.

But now it seemed as if all might be lost. One of His friends had betrayed Him. The long-smoldering hate of His opposition was about to burst into flame. No doubt His plans were carefully made for many years to come and He did not want to die. So He prayed, "If thou be willing, remove this cup from me." The great temptation of life is to follow our own desires, to make our own plans, to be guided by our own wills—and to hope God is willing.

71

But suppose God is not willing? Then we have only one of two choices: to renounce God's will and follow our own, or to renounce our own will and follow God's. And most of the time we must make that choice without fully knowing what God's will is. That requires more faith than some people have. It requires more courage than some people have. It never is an easy decision to make. Jesus' struggle was so great that sweat like great drops of blood began to pour down His face to the ground.

But He won the victory as He said, "Nevertheless not my will, but thine, be done" (Luke 22:42). But don't overlook one verse in that story: "And there appeared an angel unto him from heaven, strengthening him." If you are really sincere, God sends help when you need it most.

11

REMOVING YOUR MOUNTAINS

Every normal person wants to feel a sense of mastery over the circumstances of his own life. No person wants to feel weak and defeated. Yet, as we face up to our own personal weaknesses and the difficulties which surround us, sometimes we do feel that we are powerless and that life for us is almost hopeless.

Jesus gave us a formula for power in living. He said, "Have faith in God. For verily I say unto you, That whosoever shall say unto this mountain, Be thou removed, and be thou cast into the sea; and shall not doubt in his heart, but shall believe that those things which he saith shall come to pass; he shall have whatsoever he saith" (Mark 11:22, 23).

Look at that formula: "Faith in God"—not in ourselves, but in God. "For verily"—He emphasizes the fact that what He is about to say will be hard to believe but it is the truth. "Whosoever"—that means any person; it means me, it means you. "Say unto this mountain" that is specific and definite. Select any circumstance of your own life that is standing in your way and this formula will apply. "Be thou removed"—taken out of my way. No longer can it hurt me. "Cast into the sea"—gone forever, complete victory. "Shall not doubt . . . but shall believe"—it is through my own faith that the victory is accomplished. "Shall come to pass"—it really will happen.

There are three separate attitudes you can take in regard to Jesus' words. You can say, "It isn't true, I don't believe it." But before you say that, remember you are contradicting the most reliable book this world has ever known. Also, you are going against the wisest teacher who ever lived. Before I contradict the word of another person, I want to be sure I know more than that person. And I don't know more than Christ knew.

In the March, 1955, issue of *Reader's Digest*[1] is an article by David Sarnoff, Chairman of the Board of Radio Corporation of America and one of the most respected scientists the world has known. For nearly fifty years he has worked with scientists. In his article he states:

> In its early stages, modern science seemed at odds with religion; but this was merely a token of its immaturity. The more familiar story, in our time, is that of scientists who become increasingly aware of the mystery of the universe and come to religion through knowledge of the limitations of science. Indeed, how can those who play with the building blocks of the universe, its atoms and electrons and genes, fail to be touched by awe? Every victory of science reveals more clearly

a divine design in nature, a remarkable conformity in all things, from the infinitesimal to the infinite.

So, when I say "I don't believe in the power of faith," I am also setting myself against the testimony of the best in modern science. Science says, "Television works" and the man who believes it buys one and sees it work. Both Christ and science say, "Faith in God works," and the one who believes that tries it and sees for himself.

Jesus said if you have faith in God you can remove the mountains standing in your way. Some people don't believe that. A second attitude we can take towards the power of faith is, "I do not understand it; it is beyond me." That means neither believe nor disbelieve. It means just do nothing.

It is so easy just to surrender to life and say, "I can't do it," to accept the idea that one is weak and inferior and to fail to avail yourself of the power that you could use. Often this attitude leads one to become critical and cynical.

For a time I had associated with me at Grace Church in Atlanta a very fine Doctor of Psychology. On Sunday nights he would sit in the pulpit and study the people during the service. He told me it was one of the finest opportunities for psychological analysis one could find. He taught me some of the things to watch for in people and I have learned to spot the various types with ease. You find them in almost any congregation.

For example, there is the man who comes to church with an unbelieving attitude. He looks over the others present, thinks about what a sorry bunch of hypocrites they are. He thinks the singing is silly and he refuses to join in. Instead of giving the sermon a chance, he doubts that the minister practices what he preaches. If some person seems inspired and helped in the service, he says it is just emotionalism.

75

On the other hand, another man comes to church in an attitude of faith. He is impressed by the fact that people would freely give their money to build a beautiful house of worship. He thinks of how many people have given their very lives down through the centuries to carry the Gospel of Christ to others. Subconsciously he asks: why will a martyr die for his faith? Why has the Bible lived? What makes people pray? He is moved to believe in faith. He sings the hymns, really listens to the sermon; he responds to the voice of God in his own soul.

We recall that Jesus said, ". . . unto every one which hath shall be given; and from him that hath not, even that he hath shall be taken away from him" (Luke 19:26). That principle applies in many areas of life and especially does it apply to faith. The man who holds back his faith during the church service leaves with even less than he brought. The one who exercised his faith as best he could goes out with new strength and power.

Some don't believe in faith; some believe but feel it is beyond them; but there is a third group—they believe as best they can, they set in use what faith they do have, and as they exercise their faith they find it growing.

We are hearing much about the science of psychokinetics. It refers to the power of the human mind over conditions, circumstances, even material things. But the Bible goes further than psychokinetics. Though the Bible recognizes the power of the mind, it also recognizes the weaknesses of man. So Jesus said, "Have faith in God"—not merely in yourself. That is the faith that moves mountains.

How does one go about developing an unconquerable faith? Here are two things to do:

(1) Practice the presence of God. There are many ways to do this. For me, the best way is in church. I feel more completely the presence of God in a church service than any other place.

The building, the music, the sermon, the prayers all help. Also, in the presence of other people who are worshiping I feel support for my own worship.

I have learned to catch "moments with God" during each day. Henry Drummond, who was a spiritual genius, said, "Ten minutes spent in the presence of Christ every day, aye, two minutes, will make the whole day different."

When I drive from my home to my office at the church, I usually come into Ponce de Leon Avenue at Ponce de Leon Place. I always seem to hit a red light there and I do believe it is the slowest light to turn green in town. Then on down the hill at the ball park there is another slow light and then half a block on, still another. Then there is the one at Boulevard. I used to fuss about the delay of those four lights but now I have worked out a devotional period for them.

I have four questions I ask myself and take one at each light. First, "What am I most thankful for today?" Next, "What have I done during the past twenty-four hours of which I am ashamed?" I limit it to twenty-four hours because no traffic light is red long enough for any longer period. Usually I don't have the time to include everything even for the past day. I confess and ask God's forgiveness. At the third light I ask, "What is God's will for my life this one day?" Then at the last light I ask, "Whom should I pray for?" Every person can work out for himself moments of spiritual refreshment that make more real the presence of God.

(2) To develop faith one must simply have faith. You gain faith, not by argument but by action. We learn to trust by trusting. A lot of people try to be too intellectual in their religion. Jesus told us to love God with our minds but before that, He said we should love God with our hearts (Matt. 22:37). Before you argue about your faith, first experience it. Jesus did not give us

the reasons why faith moves mountains; He simply said, "Have faith in God."

Then He said we must get busy at the job of clearing the mountains of difficulties out of our lives. Don't wait to see if we can do it, just go ahead. And He says anyone who does not doubt "in his heart" (not mind—heart) shall gain the victory.

If there be any person reading these words who is defeated by anything, no matter what it may be, I urge you to believe right now that God's power is being released in your life. I declare to you that if you can believe right at this moment, you will now receive the strength necessary to give you complete victory. Go out on a spiritual limb and trust God with your whole heart. Rest your entire life on Him. You will find that He is able to "keep you from falling" (Jude 24).

12

PRAYER FOR CONFIDENCE IN TOMORROW

This request came in the mail: "Please tell me how to gain confidence in tomorrow and to face the future with calmness." This letter went on to say, "I realize there isn't much I can do about the past; I can work with the present; but when I think of all that might happen in the future, I feel helpless and afraid."

The first step toward a calm confidence in the future is to learn to believe that life is good. The Bible says, "We know that all things work together for good to them that love God" (Rom. 8:28). That principle applies to the future equally as it does to the present or to the past. That does not mean that everything that happens will be good. Life is composed of both joy and sorrow, victory and defeat, success and failure. And we know that tomorrow will probably bring both good and bad into our lives. Knowing that, we must think of life as a whole instead of merely separate experiences.

Here is an illustration: think of a ship. The purpose of a ship is to sail across the seas—but not all parts of the ship will float. The engine, for example, if put on the water would immediately sink. So would the propeller, the compass and many other parts of the ship. But when all the parts of the ship are securely built together, it does sail.

So with life. Some things that will happen to us are bad. Some things will be good. But when we consider all the experiences of life, carefully cementing them together with our love for God, then life as a whole will work out for good for us. And that is the faith we really want. We do not ask for the assurance that all the sorrows, disappointments, and troubles be eliminated from our tomorrows. We do not really want that.

There is a Greek legend about a woman who came to the River Styx to be carried across to the next life. Charon, the man who ran the ferry, reminded her that she could drink of the waters of Lethe, and thus forget the life she was leaving. Eagerly she said, "I will forget how I have suffered." But he pointed out, "You will also forget how you have rejoiced." "I will forget my failures," she said. "And you will forget your victories," he added. "I will forget how I have been hated," she said. "And also how you have been loved," he added. The story ends with the woman deciding it is better to retain her memory of the bad in order to retain also her memory of the good.

So it is with the future. If by drinking some magic water we could eliminate the suffering, failure, and hate of tomorrow, we would eagerly do it. But we remember that life is always two-sided and to destroy one side necessarily destroys the other side.

So we would also eliminate the joy, victory, and love. We would not drink the magic water.

Some things that happen in life are bad. Some things that happen are good. But life itself can be trusted. It is as St. Paul said: "We know that all things work together for good to them that love God." When we have that faith, we face tomorrow with hope instead of with fear.

Why do we worry about tomorrow? Not because we are afraid something bad might happen. We know there are sorrows and defeats ahead for us. Note these words of the psalmist, "Yea, though I walk through the valley of the shadow of death, I will fear no evil: for thou art with me. . . ." The psalmist knows there are valleys ahead. But underscore that word *through*. That is the reason he "will fear no evil." You can stand anything, even the deepest pain, if you know, really know, you will get through it. And how does one know? "For thou art with me." When one's life is centered in God, he knows defeat is never final. Somehow all things will work out for good.

With that faith, our fears of tomorrow give way to hope, and when we look forward with hope, life is good. One of the purest gems of all literature is Tennyson's "In Memoriam." In it you find this wonderful line, "The mighty hopes that make us men." Hope gives strength to life. In Proverbs we read, "Hope deferred maketh the heart sick: but when the desire cometh, it is a tree of life" (13:12).

Someone recently made a study of a large group of people who work in a certain office. They all did about the same work, yet, at the close of the day, some were limp with fatigue while others seemed strong and rested. It was discovered that one group had something to look forward to—a party that night, a weekend trip, something pleasant to do at home—while the other group had nothing to look forward to.

81

If you want to develop genuine hope, you must have something definite to hope for. Hope is never real until it has an object. I have suggested two questions to many hopeless people: (1) What is something you really desire in life? (2) How can you get started toward that attainment? Those two questions lead to the fixing of a goal to creative action. When we have that, we automatically eliminate most of our fears. We just do not have time to worry.

But often we feel the need of resources beyond our own strength. And that is when we turn to God and when we begin to pray. And when we really pray, words like hopeless, impossible, defeat, are eliminated from our thinking. We remember that Jesus said, "And whatsoever ye shall ask in my name, that will I do . . ." (John 14:13). That promise is so wonderful that some people just cannot believe it. But as someone has put it, "God has never broken any promise ever spoken."

"Whatsoever ye shall ask in my name, that will I do. . . ." In explanation, we must remember four facts:

(1) Frequently God has already put within our reach the "whatsoever." There was a boy who asked God to give him a good mark on his examination the next day. He prayed earnestly but he failed the exam. He lost his faith and bitterly said the promises of God were no good. The next year he decided he did not need God, he could get along by himself. So he repeated the course, studied hard, and passed the exam. It took that boy some years to realize that God had answered his prayer even before he prayed it. God had given him the mental ability to learn the course and pass the exam, but the first year he had not used God's answer. God has already given us the means to possess many of our "whatsoevers."

(2) God is wiser than we, and He has the power to distinguish between what we really want and what we think we want at the moment. One summer I rode with the junk man every day. He

82

had a fine horse and I had great fun driving. When September came I told my father I always wanted to work with the junk man and did not want to go back to school. Suppose my father had said, "All right, since you have decided what you want, you may have it"? Being wiser, he could distinguish between my immediate whims and the real desires of my heart. He refused my want but, as Tagore said, "Thou didst save me by Thy hard refusals." Fortunately for us, God answers our larger prayers even though it may require some refusals along the way.

(3) God is concerned with all His children and if my "whatsoever" conflicts with someone else's prayer, then with infinite love and wisdom, God answers the prayer that should be answered. Some time back I phoned for a plane reservation and they told me there was no chance. I prayed about it and the next day they phoned to say they had a place for me. Later I was in Dallas, Texas. I could not get a reservation back but I went on out to the airport, confidently believing I would get a seat. I sincerely asked God to help me. But the plane took off without me. I know God would have managed to get someone off that plane, but in that case, it would not have been fair.

(4) Remember these lines from our American national anthem: "Then conquer we must, when our cause it is just; And this be our motto: 'In God is our trust!'" It may be, and often is, that our "whatsoever" is not just; so, include always in prayer our Lord's words: "Nevertheless not my will, but thine, be done."

Here then is the promise: "Whatsoever ye ask in my name, if it is what you really want, and if it is in harmony with God's larger purposes and will, then you and I working together will bring it to pass." And with that assurance, we can look toward the future with confidence instead of fear.

13

OVERCOMING YOUR
INNER TENSIONS

One of the most remarkable passages in the entire Bible is Job 22:21–29. We hear a lot about the inner tensions of people. Well, Job had reasons to become tense and nervous. He had many problems.

He lost his wealth, his children died, he was sick and suffered much pain, his friends doubted his religious sincerity, even his wife turned against him. But Job worked his way through his problems to achieve great personal victory. What was the secret he found? Listen—"Acquaint now thyself with him, and be at peace. . . ."

The truth is, we are most acquainted with our *problems*. In our minds we go over our troubles again and again until every detail is sharp and clear. The mind begins to magnify our problems and make them seem larger, then with our problems growing larger, we add other ingredients to our thinking, such as resentment, self-pity, fear of worse things happening, hopelessness, and despair. And we actually work ourselves into extreme nervous tension.

But suppose that you could be certain, completely certain, that in spite of what may have happened to you or what your present state may be, in the future the following things will happen to you: Good shall come to you; you will have the financial resources to provide all your needs and more; you will have delight in living; you will accomplish the things you decide on; your prayers will be heard and answered; you will see clearly how to walk the paths of life; and when moments of depression come you will overcome them. If you really were sure those things were in your future, then would you be tense? Of course not.

The Bible promises those things. Let me give the exact words which you will find beginning with Job 22:21 ". . . good shall come unto thee . . . thou shalt be built up . . . Then shalt thou lay up gold . . . then shalt thou have thy delight . . . Thou shalt make thy prayer unto him, and he shall hear thee . . . Thou shalt also decree a thing, and it shall be established unto thee . . . the light shall shine upon thy ways."

One of the deepest laws of life is that we receive that which we expect. Jesus Himself said, ". . . believe that ye receive them, and ye shall have them" (Mark 11:24). But the important question is: How can I believe? Belief must be based on a solid foundation. That foundation is our belief in God. And that is what Job says, "Acquaint thyself with him, and be at peace." The better you become acquainted with God, the less tensions you feel and the more peace you possess.

Concluding this passage, Job says, ". . . he shall save the humble person." Before he died, someone asked Dale Carnegie the secret of his life. He said, "Every day I pray. I yield myself to God, the tensions and anxieties go out of me and peace and power come in." The trouble with many people is that they are so big in their own eyes they feel no need of God.

There are many ways to become better acquainted with God. The other day I was up in the mountains. Sitting there in the quiet coolness, my attention became fixed on a great mountain which I could see in the distance.

The peak of the mountain was obscured by a violent thunderstorm. The wind lashed it from every direction, the water poured down upon it in torrents, great bolts of lightning struck it heavy blows. I wondered if even a mountain could withstand such an onslaught. But after a while the clouds were gone and there stood the mountain glistening in the bright sunlight.

I got to thinking about what that mountain had gone through. There had been many thunderstorms, earthquakes, and fires. It had known cold winters and the heavy burdens of ice and snow. During its lifetime the wars of the world had come and gone; depressions, kings had risen and fallen, civilizations had lived and died: but the mountain is still there. Looking at it I felt stronger and more secure.

A verse of Scripture came to my mind: ". . . the strength of the hills is his also." Seeing that mountain, I became better acquainted with God. I turned to the Ninety-fifth Psalm, in which that verse is recorded, and I read the entire Psalm. It begins, "O come, let us sing unto the LORD: let us make a joyful noise." Why can we sing and be joyful? The psalmist tells us it is because of God. "For the LORD is a great God . . . the strength of the hills is his . . . The sea is his, and he made it . . ."; and triumphantly the psalmist declares, "For he is our God; and we are the people of his pasture. . . ."

One reason people get tense and nervous is because they think they do not have the resources necessary for their lives. We are driven into an attitude of defeat and fear. We shrink back from life in cowardly fashion. But when we know there is a God who truly is God, and when we know He is our God, we feel as confident and relaxed as a child in the presence of its parents.

Looking at that mountain, I thought of another verse of the Bible. ". . . If ye have faith as a grain of mustard seed, ye shall say unto this mountain, Remove hence to yonder place; and it shall remove; and nothing shall be impossible unto you" (Matt. 17:20). We become tense and worried when the mountains of life block our paths: debts we cannot pay, problems we cannot solve, obstacles we cannot overcome.

"If ye have faith"—faith in what? In yourself? That is part of the answer. Faith in other people? That, too, is part of it. But mountain-moving faith must begin in one who is bigger than the mountain. And there is One. As Job says, when we become acquainted with Him, we are at peace. Stop concentrating on your weakness and begin thinking of His strength. God isn't worried. His strength is sufficient.

The greatest Christian preacher who has ever lived said this: ". . . I have learned, in whatsoever state I am, therewith to be content" (Phil. 4:11).

The word *contentment* is derived from two Latin words: *con* and *tenio*. It means "to hold together." We use an expression, "I went to pieces." That is an exact expression because it literally happens. I have been writing about inner tension. That is what we feel when, under some strain, we do not hold ourselves together and we develop within ourselves an inner war. We have tension today in the world. What is the reason? Two or more nations are at variance with each other. The world is not unified in its purposes and desires.

When St. Paul said that he was contented, it did not mean he was satisfied with the conditions under which he lived. In fact, he was so dissatisfied that he completely gave himself in changing things. His contentment came as a result of his inner unity and singleness of purpose.

One day he was going his own hotheaded way. He was a big and important man in his own eyes. He could look after himself, he could handle his own affairs. Then suddenly he was struck down to the ground. The Bible says he began to tremble. It may not hurt you to get knocked down. It may not be bad for you to reach the point of trembling. In fact, it will do you good if it causes you to do what Paul did.

It caused him to look up and see God and realize how he had been ignoring God. It caused him to realize there was a better way to live than the way he had been living. It made him become willing to change from his ways to God's ways. So he said, "Lord, what wilt thou have me to do?" (Acts 9:6). Remember: Paul never learned contentment until first he learned consecration.

"Acquaint now thyself with him, and be at peace . . ." (Job 22:21). That is the only real and lasting answer to the inner tension and turmoil of man. After getting to know God and committing his life to God's will, Paul found the resources for a completely victorious life. He declared: "I can do all things through Christ which strengtheneth me" (Phil. 4:13). From the moment he realized that, he never knew the meaning of inner tension or of nervous worry about anything.

David had the same experience. There was a period in his life when he thought he didn't need God, but later he learned differently. After he became really acquainted with God, he said, "The LORD is my shepherd . . . surely goodness and mercy shall follow me all the days of my life" (Psalm 23). Coming to believe in God, automatically we lose our fear of tomorrow. When that happens we are at peace.

14

WHEN THERE IS PAIN IN YOUR HEART

One of the great mysteries of human life is the mystery of pain. Again and again we ask, "Why has this come to me?" Why physical sickness? Why handicaps? Why did that person die? Why must I bear this disappointment? There is the pain in our bodies, the pain in our minds, and the pain in our hearts. Why does it have to be that way, we wonder.

We can better understand the pain of life if we will keep in mind several positive facts:

(1) Every possible blessing is also a possible pain. Here is an illustration. I bought roller skates for my children. I remember that I found great joy in skating and I wanted my children to enjoy it too. However, when one puts on skates, he also greatly increases the possibility of falling and getting hurt.

I watched my children when they first tried to skate. They would fall on the hard concrete and it would hurt and sometimes they would cry. In that instance, would you say that I caused their pain? In a sense I did; but by giving them skates I also increased the possibility of joy and pleasure in their lives. By giving them skates I was allowing them to get hurt, but it certainly was not my will. It would have been very different if I had gone out and banged their heads against the concrete.

A boy is killed in an automobile wreck. When his father allowed him to drive the car he certainly did not intend that the boy be killed. The father might have said, "It is possible for one to be killed in an automobile wreck. Therefore, because I love you I will not let you drive or even ride in a car." On the other hand, the father wanted the boy to have the advantage and pleasure of the car, and thus he permitted him to drive.

God has provided for us wonderful things for our joy. Take love, for example. Love brings life's greatest blessings but it also brings life's greatest pains. God gave men and women the capacity to love each other. We marry and build our homes. Into our homes come children and then a new love is born into our hearts. Then something happens to one we love and our hearts are broken. But that is just one of the prices we must pay for love.

God gave us the capacity to dream, to hope, and to aspire. But sometimes we do not realize our dreams; our hopes are dashed to the ground; our fondest ambitions are thwarted. Then we know the pain of disappointment and frustration. On the other hand, we also have the possibility of knowing the thrill of achievement. In order to have the possibility of one we must be willing to accept the possibility of the other.

A team goes out on the baseball field to play a game. They give their best but they are beaten, and defeat is hard to bear. They could have avoided their defeat by not playing the game.

But also they would have denied themselves the chance to win. If one plays the game, then he must accept both the possibilities of winning and of losing.

Study life and you will see that life's possibilities come in pairs: goodness and evil, short and tall, strong and weak, hot and cold, black and white—and also, pain and pleasure. The existence of one carries with it the possibility of the other. If there were no pain, then there would be no pleasure in life either.

(2) Pain and suffering in this life is one of the prices we must pay for belonging to the human family. Again and again we ask, "Why do the innocent suffer?"

We have set up a court system in our land. We have judges and juries, and if a person is accused of some crime, he is given a fair trial. If found guilty, he is punished in accordance with the extent of the crime. We use great care in our courts not to punish the guiltless. But in life it doesn't work out like that.

Of course, we really admit that sin brings suffering both here and in the hereafter, but it is also true that some who have suffered the most were innocent. Here is a father and mother who have lived righteously and yet their son or daughter goes astray and breaks their hearts. Some of the finest saints are made to lie on beds of pain. Some of the most consecrated lives must bear burdens of great disappointment.

But if we insist that God set up the world on an individual basis—allowing each one to suffer merely to the extent of his own wrongdoing—then we must also restrict all our joys to those we can bring upon ourselves. Look into your own life and see how much you enjoy which came through the efforts of others. Then ask if you would like to give up all those things.

For example, take your automobile. Could you make one by yourself? Then, even if you could, you would have to go out and dig an oil well for yourself and refine the oil into petrol. Then you would have to build some roads to drive it on. You see, just in your own effort, an automobile is completely impossible. You use electricity. Would you be able to discover it, generate it, wire your home, make a light bulb, refrigerator, washing machine, television set, and all the other things you have?

Suppose you get sick? If you lived in an individual world, you could call no physician. There would be no hospital to which you could be carried and no nurse to give sympathetic care. The medicines which brilliant and dedicated men have discovered would not be available to you. And when you died you would not even be buried.

We enjoy a multitude of blessings which we did not cause. And in the same way we suffer many pains that are not our fault. Sometimes people say to me, "What have I done to deserve this?" and often the answer is "Nothing." Neither have you done anything to deserve many of your blessings. It is all part of belonging to the great human family. We suffer for the sins of each other.

Now here I come to a mystery. Why does God seem to intervene for certain individuals and not for others? I, myself, have prayed for certain people and have seen miraculous answers come. I prayed the other day for a lady with cancer and almost immediately her pain went away and it looks now as if a miracle has happened in her life. Yet, I have prayed for others and it seemed to make no difference. Why one and not the other?

(3) We may be sure that God is working with us to help us overcome the pain of body, mind, and heart in our lives. The psalmist put two wonderful statements together: "He healeth the broken in heart, and bindeth up their wounds. He telleth the number of stars; he calleth them all by their names" (Ps. 147:3, 4). That is, the God of the universe is also the God of the person.

And God works with us in many different ways. Sometimes He works directly with the individual and takes away his pain. Sometimes God waits until the prayer can be answered for His entire family of children. If you are a parent, you doubtless have prayed that your child be saved from the paralysis of polio. And now our hearts have been thrilled with the news that God seems to have answered that prayer for all the children. Maybe God was waiting for a man like Dr. Jonas E. Salk, through whom He could answer that prayer.

Sometimes God answers our prayer, not by eliminating the pain, but by giving us the strength to bear it. I was in Wilmington, North Carolina, for a week. One afternoon I drove out to the beach and there I saw a scene of destruction. It was not long ago that a hurricane hit that beach and destroyed hundreds of houses. I saw many of them torn to pieces. But also I saw many homes that were left standing without harm. Some of the houses were built of flimsy and cheap material while others were built with strength enough to withstand the storm. The storm revealed the character of the houses.

And that happens in life. The purpose of Christ was not to eliminate all the storms of life. He did not come to teach people how to have a good time and to avoid trouble. He came to create character. To His disciples He said, ". . . In the world ye shall have tribulation; but be of good cheer; I have overcome the world" (John 16:33). And through His grace, we too, can overcome our worlds.

Dr. W. A. Smart tells of a father who brought his little girl to the doctor. She had cut her eyelid. The doctor needed to take some stitches but for some reason did not wish to use an anesthetic. He asked the little girl if she could keep from jumping when he used the needle. She answered, "I can, if Daddy will hold my hand." And she did not flinch once.

What good did holding her father's hand do? That did not lessen the number of stitches to be taken, neither did it lessen the pain. Yet, if her father had not been there it would have made all the difference in the world.

That simple illustration suggests to us the experiences of thousands of God's children. There is a Father, strong, wise, and loving, into whose hand we can slip our hands. Then, no matter how dark or painful the way, we can bear the pain without flinching and, even in the midst of the pain, we find peace and victory.

15

WHEN YOU ARE
DISAPPOINTED

A minister comes to know the innermost secrets of many hearts, and deep down in nearly every heart he finds a disappointment of some kind. Even the most successful among us have dreams that are never realized and hopes that are never fulfilled. Something we have planned and worked for eludes our grasp, some cherished possession is taken away. If one doesn't learn to handle disappointment, eventually life turns sour and there is no joy left in it.

The best words I have heard spoken about disappointment are these: "I have learned to turn disappointments into *His* appointments." That doesn't mean that in the face of tragedy we piously fold our hands and say, "Well, it is the will of God, and I must bear it." It could be that your disappointment is the will of God. Even if it is, that doesn't mean we should resign ourselves to it and stop there.

St. Paul advises, ". . . and having done all, to stand" (Eph. 6:13). He doesn't say, "And having done all, give up and quit." He says, "stand." That signifies continued action on your part. You are traveling down a certain roadway in life. Suddenly a block is in your way. It may be God saying, "I cannot let you go further that way," but that is never God's final word. He may say, "I have another way for you." God's way never comes to a dead end. He may change our direction but there is always an open road for us.

Here is an illustration. Once there lived in Decatur, Illinois, a boy who was deeply interested in photography. He carefully saved his money to buy a certain book and happily he ordered it. The publisher, however, made a mistake in his order and instead of sending the book on photography, he sent a book on ventriloquism. This boy was not interested in ventriloquism. In fact, he did not even know what it was.

He didn't know he could send the book back and probably he didn't have the money for postage, anyway. He could have put the book aside and nursed his disappointment. Instead, he began reading it and he became interested. He learned to throw his voice and eventually got a wooden dummy which he named Charlie McCarthy. Out of a disappointment, Edgar Bergen built a great career. Now I ask the question: Was it a mistake of the publisher or was it the providential hand of God that he was sent the wrong book? Who can say? And in the face of our disappointments, before we resign ourselves to hopeless despair, let us ask, Is this disappointment *His* appointment?

At the age of forty-eight, Victor Hugo was banished to the island of Guernsey to live for twenty years in lonely exile. It was a bitter disappointment—but there he wrote *Les Miserables,* one of the greatest novels of all time. Without the disappointment, his best work would never have been accomplished. Where does accident end and God's providence begin? Who can tell?

It has been said that every man's life is a diary in which he means to write one story, and is forced to write another. That is, we plan for one way; we are forced to travel another. Here is a fine illustration of that fact: Writing to the church in Rome, St. Paul says, "Whensoever I take my journey into Spain, I will come to you . . ." (Rom. 15:24).

To go to Spain was his dream and his plan. It was a thrilling and challenging adventure to which his soul responded. In his heart was the spirit of Kipling's explorer: "Something lost behind the Ranges. Lost and waiting for you. Go!" Instead of that great trip into Spain, he landed in a cold and dirty prison cell in Rome. Instead of the glory of conquest for Christ in faraway places, he was forced to face a prison wall and beyond that—execution and death.

We dream of conquests in some Spain but many end up in some prison house of life, chained, confined, and disappointed. In one of John Masefield's poems, "The Widow in the Bye Street," is the story of a widow who made a living sewing shrouds for the dead. It was hard work and little pay. To provide the bare necessities for herself and her son, she must work from early morning to late at night. But while she worked, she dreamed.

Some day her son would become a man. He would be a fine man and would succeed in life. Then he would be able to provide comforts for her in her old age. With that dream to support her, she worked even harder and gave him every advantage. The boy did grow up but he fell in love with an unworthy woman. One day he found her with another man and he killed that man.

The long arm of the law found him, tried him, and sentenced him to death. He was hung in disgrace.

The widowed mother goes back again to sewing shrouds, her dreams broken. She faces the dull, grey walls of her prison of loneliness, desolation, and disappointment. I cannot believe that her disappointment was God's will. I do believe, however, that even in the circumstance which life had so cruelly forced upon her, there was still a good way to be found.

It is hard to believe that Paul's prison was God's appointment. It represented the cruelty and heartlessness of man. But whether it was God's plan or not, because Paul was what he was, he turned his disappointment into God's appointment. He might have cursed his fate, raved against his jailers, become bitter and rebellious. Or he might have said, "I have done my best but I was . blocked, so I will surrender to the will of God and sit here without complaint." He took neither course. Instead, he followed his own admonition to others: ". . . and having done all, to stand." He turned to God and in so doing he transformed and glorified his imprisonment and triumphantly he wrote: "I Paul, the prisoner of Jesus Christ . . ." (Eph. 3:1).

Paul dreamed of going to Spain. Instead, he landed in a Roman prison, but instead of crying out against God or piously folding his hands and doing nothing, Paul dedicated himself, even in prison. Later he wrote: "But I would ye should understand, brethren, that the things which happened unto me have fallen out rather unto the furtherance of the gospel" (Phil. 1:12).

Certainly every guard in the prison who came in contact with him was never quite the same again. If he could not preach to the multitudes in Spain, he would preach to the guards in prison. If he could not have the opportunities he wanted, he would take the opportunities he had. When you pick up your New Testament, notice how many of the books were written by Paul. Much of his best writing was done while in prison. There he found the quietness that he could not have found on his missionary journeys. I have no idea what victories he might have won in Spain, but I doubt if his contribution to the cause of Christ in Spain would have meant as much to the Christian world as have those letters he wrote while in prison. Paul's prison might have been God's will after all. His disappointment might have been God's appointment. Certainly Paul made it so, anyway.

But what shall we say of those crushing disappointments in life which do not turn into good fortune? Not every prison door opens out into centuries of service, not all valleys of the shadow of death lead to the brightness of the morning. Some of our disappointments we are forced to live with all the way. What then? To live with a broken body, a broken heart, a broken life brings fresh suffering with the dawning of each new day. What then?

Here we must go deeper than the success stories we read in magazines, deeper than those quick and easy formulas on "how to be happy." We must go to the cross on Calvary's hill. Without the cross, Christ would not have been the Savior. And when we are tempted to despondency and despair, let us hear the Voice across the centuries calling, ". . . take up the cross, and follow me" (Mark 10:21).

Dr. Wallace Hamilton tells of an old grandfather clock which stood for generations faithfully ticking off the time. Its momentum came from a heavy weight, suspended by a double chain. In pity the owner thought, "Too bad that such an old clock should have to bear so great a load." So he removed the weight, but the ticking stopped. The clock pleaded, "Please put my weight back. That is what keeps me going."

It may be you have missed some Spain you dreamed of and ended up in some prison of disappointment. If you can't get out of your prison, let God help you make something out of it. Instead of letting disappointment be the end of everything, work to make it the beginning of something, remembering how God used a cross even for the salvation of the world.

16

WHEN YOU HAVE FAILED

For some years I have studied the problems of people. In a sense, every problem is different because every person is different but basically there are only four problems—they are fear, guilt, self-centeredness, and the inability to forget. Take that last one—it is one of the hardest to deal with.

A young lady was talking to me about the death of her mother. She seemed grief-stricken and I tried to explain where her mother is now and to give her some of the assurances of eternal life from the Bible. But quickly she told me that wasn't her difficulty. Now that her mother was gone, she remembered unkind things she said to her. She recalled times when she might have been kinder and more helpful toward her mother. Now she remembered with regret and shame.

Well, we all have things we would like to forget. And, if we can't forget, life becomes an intolerable burden. Let me give a formula to use in meeting this problem and an illustration of how it works. Both are found in the Bible. The formula is: "... this one thing I do, forgetting those things which are behind, and reaching forth unto those things which are before, I press toward the mark ..." (Phil. 3:13, 14).

Now for the illustration (John 20:19–23): It involves eleven men. There were twelve but one was so completely overwhelmed by his unhappy memories that he committed suicide. The other eleven were gathered together. If misery loves company, then these men loved being together that night. They were in the depths of despair. In my mind I can hear them talking:

"I had a good fishing business and had worked hard to pay for my boat but Jesus came along and asked me to go with Him. I didn't mind the financial sacrifices because I believed we could win the world in His name. But now I've lost everything." That is Simon Peter talking. "Yes," speaks up Matthew, "I was doing mighty well in my job as tax collector. In another year or so I would have been comfortable." And so the talk goes. And people today look back on decisions they made, maybe a financial investment or some other venture of faith, only to lose everything and feel they have nothing to start over on again.

Also, those eleven disciples felt shame. They lost their nerve, they didn't "quit themselves like men." They deserted as cowards. Matthew recalls, "Then all the disciples forsook him, and fled" (Matt. 26:56). It isn't so bad to fail when one has done his best but when we remember our failures with shame, it doubles the bitterness of our memories.

We remember when we surrendered our ideals, when we violated the laws of God, when we betrayed the trust of our loved ones. Many of us can understand how the disciples felt.

The eleven disciples were gathered in a room. Jesus had been crucified and now they felt both despair and shame. Not only that, they were afraid. "Keep that door locked," they would whisper. Any little noise in the hallway would drive new fear into their hearts. They would like to go out and start over again but they were afraid to try.

Vast numbers of people today feel exactly this same fear. Having failed in some way and feeling remorse and shame, fear grips our lives. We lose our will power, our determination, our courage. Because of fear, we draw into some shell and quit without trying to make a comeback.

Also, these eleven men not only felt despair, shame, and fear because of their failure, they also felt Christ-forsaken. They had enjoyed so much the friendship of Christ. They remembered how He calmed the storm that night and how comforting was His presence. They remembered His kind words of encouragement, the radiance of His personality, His wonderful plans for the world. Now He is dead.

A man told me, "I can't pray any more." I asked him if he ever could pray. He sat silent a few moments and tears began to flow down his cheeks. He told me how his mother taught him to pray, "Now I lay me down to sleep." He told me about joining the church and working in it. He told me how he and his wife used to have prayer together. "Now," he said, "I have lost God."

We remember how David missed the way. He looked back at some things he had done with regret and shame, and he realized he was losing God. Frantically he cried out, "Cast me not away from thy presence and take not thy holy spirit from me" (Ps. 51:11).

As long as these eleven men had hanging over them the ugly shadow of yesterday's failure, they would be hopelessly defeated by despair, shame, fear, and a sense of Christ-forsakenness. They wanted to forget it all, but how could they! Just to say, "I'll forget something," is not enough. The only way to expel one thought from our minds is by substituting a more powerful thought. St. Paul recognized that fact. He said, ". . . forgetting those things which are behind . . ." but he didn't stop there. He further said, ". . . reaching forth unto those things which are before" (Phil. 3:13).

Just as faith conquers fear and love conquers hate, so positive action overcomes past failures. We should learn to stop keeping company with our failures. It is so easy to hold in our minds some miserable yesterday—to nurse it, nurture it, and brood over it and eventually to surrender to it. On the other hand, there is a better way.

When they first manufactured golf balls, they made the covers smooth. Then it was discovered that after a ball had been roughed up, one could get more distance out of it. So they started manufacturing them with dimpled covers. So it is with life. It takes some rough spots in your life to make you go your farthest.

Tom Paine was an agnostic who lived in the days of the American Revolution. But at Valley Forge he did say one good thing. He said, "Let us thank God for this crisis for it gives us the opportunity to prove that we are men."

Recently I was in another state to speak at an institution maintained for veterans of various American wars. There I had an audience of 2,700 men. I was totally unprepared for the task. Most of these men were sixty years old and above. I spoke in an auditorium which seated 1,200 and they filled it to capacity.

The other 1,500 men listened over the speaker system. They were confined to their rooms. Many of them were blind, large numbers were confined to wheel chairs, even more were helpless bed patients. A death a day is average there. I looked at a large hillside covered with little white crosses.

The man in charge told me that for the most part these are forgotten men. He told me that many of them go an entire year without ever receiving a letter. I had to be careful to leave out of my sermons any reference to home and family and children. These men had lost that. I couldn't preach about another chance at life, for there was no other chance for them. About all they had to look forward to was to lie beneath one of those little crosses on the side of that hill. And there would be nobody to shed a tear at their passing.

As I sought to minister to those men, I thought of many other people I have known. People who have had setbacks and disappointments but, thank God, they also have another chance at life. I thought about how foolish a man is who, having that chance, refuses it and instead lets the bitterness of some unhappy yesterday ruin his life.

I thought of the night Christ walked into the presence of His disciples who had failed and who were filled with despair, shame, fear, and a sense of forsakenness. Notice carefully how the Lord handled these men. First, He said, "Peace be unto you." He wanted to get the panic out of their minds. To let them be still and think. Next, ". . . he shewed unto them his hands and his side." He wanted them to know He was still living, that God had not been defeated. Not one word did He speak of their failure. After all, nothing now could be done about it so He wanted them just to forget it. God is always eager to forget and helps us forget that yesterday is gone beyond our reach. If nothing can be done about it, it is foolish to keep thinking about it.

St. Paul said, ". . . forgetting those things which are behind, and reaching forth unto those things which are before. . . ." The only satisfactory way to forget is to reach forth. Jesus looked into the faces of these fearful failures and said, ". . . as my Father hath sent me, even so send I you." He gave them a new goal to strive for, a new task to work at. And He did more than that: ". . . he breathed on them, and saith unto them, Receive ye the Holy Ghost" (John 20:22).

Not only does He give us the task, He also gives us the power. And with Him as our companion, we can forget past failures because we can be sure that success lies ahead.

17

WHEN YOU GET
THE BLUES

H ere is a question from the Bible which all of us have asked
many times: "Why art thou cast down, O my soul? and why
art thou disquieted within me?" That is, why do I get blue and
discouraged? Why do I get upset inside? The psalmist asked the
identical question three times in Psalms 42 and 43. We have
asked that question many more times than thrice.

One reason we become "cast down" and "disquieted" is
because of an inferiority complex, a shrinking shyness that makes
us feel inadequate. We struggle with self-doubt until it takes our
strength and saps our nerves. Harold Sherman tells of a boy who
nearly drowned. As a result he became afraid of water and would
never go swimming again. As he grew older, he would use such
expressions as "That is over my head," or "This is too deep for

me," or "If I tried that I would be sunk." Many people live with a shrinking, shy, failure attitude toward life. Such an attitude brings periods of deep depression to us.

Periods when we are "disquieted" and "cast down" are part of the natural rhythm of life. I speak often of the tides because I believe that the law of the tides is a basic pattern of all life. The tides rise and fall, the tides go out and they come back. We have moments of exhilaration and moments of depression. There is an upbeat and a downbeat in moods of human beings. No person lives on a perfectly even keel. In the words of the old spiritual, "Sometimes I'm up, sometimes I'm down."

A man was talking to me about the chart which determines the hours of the day when fish are active and will bite better. It is published on the sports pages and is called the "Solunar Fishing Guide." He told me it applies equally to human beings, that at certain hours we feel more active and that we should plan our work to take advantage of those active moments. I've been studying it and I believe there is something to it. I've noticed that people are more responsive in some church services than others. Instead of having church at a certain hour, maybe we should plan to take advantage of the hours when people will be most responsive.

But the problem is not these normal fluctuations of the human spirit; the problem occurs when we get into periods of depression and inner turmoil and can't seem to rise again. Someone quotes an interview with Cy Young, the great baseball pitcher. He won more ball games than any other pitcher who ever lived. In talking about it, he said: "Back when I played, if a pitcher got into trouble out on the mound, the manager didn't rush out to talk with us or send in a relief. We just had to keep on pitching and pitch our way out of trouble." He went on to explain, "If I were off form, I'd keep on pitching until I got in form again."

So it is in life. There are no relief pitchers to get us out of a jam. We just have to keep on pitching until we work ourselves out. We shouldn't just surrender to our moods of depression.

When you feel as the psalmist expressed, "Why art thou cast down, O my soul? and why art thou disquieted within me?" you can pull out of your periods of discouragement and depression. Down in Florida the other day a young man who flies jet planes told me their greatest danger in pulling out of a dive was blacking out. So it is in life. When our spirits are diving downward, it is easy to "black out" instead of "pull out." But you will never "black out" if you will emphasize these four things:

(1) Never forget that you are important. No person created in the image of God is useless. Maybe you have not found the place in life that you want most, maybe your life doesn't seem big. But heaven has bestowed upon you a personality, one that no one else can duplicate. You were born for two worlds—this one and the one to come. You have been made only "a little lower than the angels" and you have been "crowned . . . with glory and honour" (Psalm 8:5).

Because of who you are and what you are, you can afford to believe in yourself and depend on yourself. You are easily upset when you lean on other people, but when you have learned to balance yourself on your own feet, you develop a stimulating independence. If God had wanted you to imitate someone else, He would not have made you in the first place. Never let yourself forget that you are a person God made and wanted at this time.

(2) In times when your soul is "cast down," when "you are discouraged, thinking all is lost," remember that you are needed. There is at least one important work to be done that will not be done unless you do it. We all give ourselves to something. Many people give themselves to something that is beneath them. Jesus

109

said, ". . . ye are of more value than many sparrows" (Matt. 10:31), yet many people give themselves to nothing higher than what a sparrow gives himself to—just eating, sleeping, and the routines of daily life. In times of depression, think bigger thoughts of what your life can amount to.

(3) When you get the blues, remember that there are several people in you. You are a good person, but you are also evil. You shrink back from life, but you also face a hard situation with calmness and courage. You have temptations to sink into some mudhole of living, but you also reach for the stars. Within you lives one who is careless and doesn't care, another who is greedy and selfish, another who is controlled by his passions, and many other selves. But never forget, within you there is always a best self.

You are the ruler over these various selves, just as a king is ruler over his kingdom. But sometimes we let one of these selves take charge of us and we lose control. The Bible says, ". . . he that ruleth his spirit [is better] than he that taketh a city" (Prov. 16:32). So when you are abnormally depressed and discouraged, it means you have let one of your inner selves gain control over you. You need to rise up and assert your authority. Never give up. You can always do something about yourself.

(4) The psalmist tells how to pull out of those times when you feel depressed and discouraged. He says, "Hope thou in God." When you believe in God, you have hope; as the sun drives the clouds away, so hope chases away our blues.

One of the closest friends of Jesus was John the Baptist. They were cousins and probably played together as boys. One day the news came that John had been murdered. Surely it grieved the heart of the Lord and it was enough to discourage Him. What did He do? The Bible tells us ". . . he went up into a mountain apart to pray: and when the evening was come, he was there alone" (Matt. 14:23).

The other night I was on one of those big airliners. The plane began to be tossed rather violently. Then the pilot's voice came over the speakers. He said, "Friends, we are entering a slight turbulence." (They always say "slight turbulence," but up there I don't think of any turbulence as slight.) He said, "We are now flying at 15,000 feet. We are going up to 21,000 feet to get over the weather." The big plane turned upwards and soon there was smooth flying again.

And when we hit these turbulent spots in life, if we look up toward the heavens and get closer to God, it is wonderful how things smooth out. That is what Jesus did when His friend died. He did it other times, when life was hard and discouraging. Even at the very last, he went out into the Garden to be alone with the Father. And when a person has a firm hold on God's hand, he has the power and strength flowing into him to keep him on his feet.

I read an article recently about a metal called permaloy. It is a highly magnetic substance, but it acts in a strange way. When lying in certain directions, it has no magnetic power. But when it is placed in direct line with the magnetic pull of the earth, its power is very strong. The same is true in our own lives. When we are out of line with the magnetic pull of Almighty God, we have no strength, we lose our grip. That is when we are frustrated and feel discouraged. But when our lives are lined up in right relationship with God, we have the ability to reach out, to grasp hold, and to conquer life.

Almighty God meant for us to walk on earth as men and not shrink back in fear from life. Basil King wrote this wonderful line, "Be bold and mighty forces will come to your aid." There are times when the highest form of prayer is action. When you have felt God's presence and your soul is reassured, then it is time to act. Maybe you can only see one step ahead, but as you take that step you will feel new heart and strength. A cast down, disquieted soul cannot live within one who has talked to God and has begun some action. Mighty forces do come to the aid of one who is bold.

18

WHEN YOU ARE HANDICAPPED

"There was given to me a thorn in the flesh" said St. Paul (2 Cor. 12:7). The fact is: every person can make that same statement. Where is there one who does not have something that holds him or her back? Something that keeps us from reaching all the goals in life our hearts are set upon.

I preached some time ago through an interpreter to four hundred children who were deaf. Most of them were born that way. Others are born crippled and never know what it is to walk normally. Some are born emotionally handicapped and are never able to become smoothly flowing personalities. Some are born with the capacity to dream and with large ambitions, but later realize they do not have the abilities to achieve those ambitions.

113

Some lack opportunity; others have suffered some tragic accident or disease.

Recently I was in a preaching mission in a city in which is located a university. Many of the students wanted to talk with me but my schedule was so crowded I first said I did not have time. They were so eager, however, that I told them I would come to the campus each night at eleven o'clock and those who wished could meet me in one of the large parlors there. Each night many would come and we would discuss the questions of life. One of their first interests was love and marriage. All normal young people want that. But as we talked, I realized some of them would be disappointed. Some of them would never find true love and a happy home and those would go through life disappointed.

Well, in one way or another, all of us miss something we would like to have. Every person must face some blockade along the pathway to happiness and success in life. When that blockade blocks your progress, what can you do about it? You can hurdle the handicap that would hold you back if you will take a positive attitude. But that is hard. Much easier it is to surrender to some negative attitude such as rebellion or self-pity. The most remarkable thing about Paul's "thorn in the flesh" is that we do not know what it is. We have thirteen letters written by him in which he has much to say about the cross of Christ and the burdens of Christians. He writes about the hardships in establishing the Kingdom of God. He tells us much about suffering. But it seems he never had time to explain his own handicap.

He was so busy with his work, so concerned about his mission, that he looked beyond that which would have held him back and he kept going. He did not want that "thorn." Three times he prayed that it might be removed. But if he had to live with it, then live with it he would and get on with the main business of his life.

114

A great violinist was giving a concert when the A string on his violin broke. Without hesitating he transposed the music and finished the concert on three strings. A lesser violinist might have stopped and moaned about his bad luck. But it takes a great artist to say, "If I can't play on four strings, I will play on three."

So it is in life. Hardly any person has all he would like to have. We can complain about our bad luck, or we can go ahead and produce melody with what we have.

One of the secrets of success and happiness in life is being willing to accept ourselves as we are. You could not choose who your parents would be. You had nothing to say about the color of your skin, whether you would be a man or woman, whether you would be short or tall. A pine tree will be a pine tree until it dies and goes back to dust. It can never be anything else.

So it is with each of us. We are not responsible for being the persons we are. God made us who we are and that is fixed forever. We might wish God had made us differently, but no amount of wishing can make much change. Thus, our business in life is to take ourselves in hand and see what we can make out of the selves we are. And in spite of our limited and handicapped selves, we can make a contribution to the world.

I once was in a preaching mission with Dr. James H. Robinson of New York. He is one of the really great preachers of America today and I found it very difficult to try to preach from the same platform with him. He was born a Negro in the slums of Knoxville, Tennessee. One night he told our congregation of several thousand people about his early resentments.

As a young man he would sit on the steps of Knoxville's public library and watch white people walk past who didn't want to go in. He wanted to go in, his whole being cried out for a chance to read and learn, but he was a Negro and the doors were closed to him. He came to hate the white people of Knoxville so that he would sit and look at the high water tower and wish he could poison every white person there. He said there were three reasons he did not do it: he didn't have the poison, he was afraid to climb high places, and he never could figure how he could keep from drinking the same water.

He wanted to go to college. All his people told him he was nothing but a Negro and there was no chance for him. But he left home one day to go to school. His parents gave him one dollar. That is all the help his own people ever gave him. He has outgrown his resentment. Today he has a Ph.D. degree and he has become a truly great man ministering to the hearts of many people.

I read of a young man who one summer sold books from house to house. He was lame and walked with great difficulty. At one house where he stopped, the lady rudely turned him down. When he started away she saw his lameness and called him back. "I didn't know you were lame," she said, "I will buy a book." He wasn't selling sympathy, he was selling books, and he let her know it. She said, "Doesn't being lame color your life?" He made a wonderful reply: "Yes, but thank God I can choose the color."

When life is not all we want, some choose the color of blue which stands for a depressed, despondent spirit. Some choose the color of yellow. They run away from life in a cowardly fashion. But others choose red, which stands for courage. "Yes, thank God, I can choose the color."

In Switzerland there is a town by the name of End der Welt. In English it means "End of the world." It is surrounded by high mountains and the road into it suddenly stops on the farther side of the town before an impassable rocky cliff. When a man gets there, he feels he can go no further. But hidden away in that rocky cliff is a narrow path that leads up the mountain to the heights above. If one searches diligently, he can find that path and go on.

At some time in life, nearly every person arrives at a place which seems to be the "end of the world." We remember Miss Haversham in Dickens' *Great Expectations*. Elaborate preparations had been made for her wedding but her lover jilted her. In grief and humiliation, Miss Haversham closed all the blinds of the house, stopped every clock, left the wedding cake on the table to gather cobwebs, and continued to wear her wedding dress until it hung in yellow decay about her shrunken form. Her disappointment became her end of the world.

I read about a traveler who fell down the side of a mountain and was knocked unconscious. Finally he woke up but he had no idea how long he had been there. He had lost all sense of time and direction. He looked across the valley and saw the sun just above the horizon, but he could not tell whether the sun was rising or setting. For the first time he realized that, rising or setting, the sun looks the same.

So it is in life—these experiences come upon us that change our lives. Sometimes our fondest dreams are thwarted. We are very conscious of our weaknesses and limitations. It is so easy to feel that everything is lost, that life from now on will not be worth living. But it may be—it often is—that which we thought was the setting of the sun may be the sunrise. There may be more light ahead than we thought possible. What seemed to be the end may be a new beginning.

There is a painting which shows the devil at a chessboard with a young man. The devil has just made his move and the young man's king is in check. On his face is written defeat and despair. One day Paul Morphy, the great chess genius, stood looking at that painting. Carefully he studied the positions on the board. Suddenly his face lighted up and he shouted to the young man in the painting, "You still have a move—don't give up, you still have a move."

We come to those moments when it seems we are check-mated, we see no winning move we can make. Then the great Master of all life comes closer to us. He remembers one day when He prayed to be spared from the cross. "Let this cup pass from me . . ." He pleaded. The cross seemed the end of His world. But there was still another move. Beyond the cross was an empty tomb—and victory. That same Christ can see beyond your cross to some triumph. "Don't give up, you still have a move," He says.

19

WHEN TEARS ARE FLOWING

One of the great things about Jesus was that He spent more time reading people than He did books. His sermons came out of real life. He saw a shepherd looking for a lost sheep, a merchant buying pearls, a tenant farmer plowing in the field, a lily growing by the wayside, a sparrow falling to the earth—and He used these scenes from daily life to show the eternal truths of God.

I was in Miami for a series of services. Thousands of people were there on vacation seeking a good time. One night, while walking down one of the brightly lighted streets, I passed a Western Union office. It was deserted except for the clerk and one lady. She had a telegram in her hand and was crying her heart out. In a land of soft moonbeams and sea breezes, hearts can still be broken.

I stood there a few moments and then walked on, but I kept thinking about her. Had she been physically ill, she could have gone to a physician and he would have helped her. Suppose she had seen me and said, "You are a minister. My heart is broken. Tell me how to dry my tears." Many have said that to me. Whenever I speak about sorrows and heartaches in the paper, on the radio, or on television, my mail greatly increases and the telephone rings more often. Many times a preacher is driven to his knees, seeking a wisdom greater than his own.

Had that lady in Miami spoken to me, I might have said, "Suffering is caused by sin. You have not been living right and now God is punishing you. You should get on your knees and repent." I have said that to some and I have seen the forgiveness of God take away the pain and bring back a song into a heart. But many times that is not the answer.

I might have said to her, "Your suffering is just in your mind. Things aren't as bad as they seem. Get your mind on something else. Get out and walk on the beach, look at the moon, listen to the gentle splashing of the waves." Sometimes that is the answer. We brood over some slight hurt until it seems much worse than it really is. But that is not always the answer. Pain can be very real. Someone wrote a little poem:

> There was a faith-healer of Deal
> Who said, "Although pain isn't real
> When I sit on a pin
> And it punctures my skin
> I dislike what I fancy I feel."

I might have told that lady, "Suffering is part of the business of living, and you will just have to brace yourself and take it." A little girl once fell down on the pavement and skinned

120

her knee. She said to her mother, "Wouldn't it be good if the whole world were cushioned?" But the world isn't cushioned and sometimes we can fall down and get hurt.

I might have said to that lady, "Suffering is good for you. Just as the cold north winds drive the roots of the oak tree deeper into the ground, so can your troubles strengthen your soul and develop your life."

Had she spoken to me I might have told her about the belief of a primitive African tribe. They believe that, although God wishes good for all His children and tries to make them happy, He has a half-witted brother who thwarts God's plans and gets in God's way. I believe there is a Devil and he does cause a lot of heartache, but that isn't the answer.

What is the answer?

Had that lady asked me to dry her tears, to begin with, I would have urged her to go ahead and cry. Some people have a foolish attitude that one should never give way to grief. But God made us with the ability to cry and tears are part of the normal operation of nature, a safety valve that God provided. To keep our grief shut up inside is a mistake. I would warn the lady, however, that crying is not the full answer and that crying can be overdone.

Then I would have sought to learn the cause of her tears. Maybe she was lonely. Seeing so many others having a good time but not knowing anyone, she might have found it hard to be by herself. Many hearts are saddened by loneliness. Maybe she was broke. Having saved all year for a vacation, she might have found it cost more than she anticipated. Financial strains do cause pain in the heart.

Maybe she had just received a telegram telling her that someone she loved very dearly had died. Maybe there was trouble in her marriage. The one she loved she might have lost. Maybe she could see no hope in her future and was overwhelmed by life. Whatever the cause, I would have talked with her about it and together we would have thought about what we could do to remedy the situation. No situation is hopeless. There is a solution to every problem.

But as we talked, somewhere in the conversation I would have opened to her the Word of God. Ernie Pyle, the famous war correspondent, wrote a wonderful story of a walk on the beaches of Normandy after that invasion. The sand was strewn with the personal effects of the boys who lay fallen in battle—snapshots, letters, books. By the side of one boy there was a guitar. Near another he saw a Bible half buried in the sand. Ernie Pyle picked it up and walked on. When he had gone half a mile, he turned back and laid it beside the boy where he had found it.

He said, "I don't know why I picked it up, or why I put it back." Maybe he picked it up thinking he would send it to the boy's parents. It would be a comfort to them. Maybe he put it back feeling that since the boy had died with his Bible, it ought to remain with him forever.

Whatever the reason, that experience indicates man's feeling that the Bible has the answer for the needs of human life. To this lady I might have read, "And God shall wipe away all tears from their eyes; and there shall be no more death, neither sorrow, nor crying, neither shall there be any more pain . . ." (Rev. 21:4). Or I might have talked to her about this: "Let not your heart be troubled: ye believe in God, believe also in me" (John 14:1).

But to her whose heart had been broken, I would especially recommend the seventh verse of Psalm 28: "The LORD is my strength and my shield; my heart trusted in him, and I am helped: therefore my heart greatly rejoiceth; and with my song will I praise him."

We need to remind ourselves frequently that there is such a Being as God—a creative, infinite, personal Being—One who brought this universe into existence, who sustains it with His power, who knows all that happens to each of His children. "The LORD is my strength"—that enables one to keep going, no matter what happens.

The other day I flew over the Okefenokee Swamp. We were down low and I could see an ugly green film over the water. It looked dirty and unclean—a breeding place for health-destroying creatures. At one time the water in that swamp was sweet and pure, coming from clear springs high in the mountains. But in that low place it had stopped, and having stopped it had stagnated.

So in life. If you stop when you hit low places, your life begins to stagnate. Sometimes tears blind our eyes and we can't see the way ahead, but we must keep going. A physician will explain to you that you use different parts of the brain for different purposes. You use the upper brain cells when you worry and brood. Fear also is in the upper brain cells. The lower brain cells control the muscular activities of your body. Thus, when you engage in activity, it takes the usual strain off the upper brain cells and allows them to function normally.

In New England, when a person has great sorrow and pain in his heart, someone will probably say to him, "Go out and tell it to the bees." That is a fine thing to do. We say, "As busy as a bee." As one watches the unceasing activity of the bees, it stimulates the lower brain cells to work, thus relieving the tension that a broken heart causes.

When your heart is broken and tears fill your eyes, your first inclination may be to go to bed, to give up in surrender. But as you fill your mind with God and exercise faith in God, His power flows into you, a power which demands expression. And as you keep going, you become able to handle that ache in your heart.

The psalmist said, "My heart trusted in him . . . and with my song will I praise him." Recently there was a popular song, "Just Walking in the Rain." Several years ago, there was another popular song, "Singing in the Rain." The two go together: when the rain comes into your life and everything seems dark and dreary, keep walking—don't stop. And as you walk, you will begin to sing. We can't prevent the rain from coming. But through faith in God and with His power working in us and for us we can learn to sing in the rain.

"My heart greatly rejoiceth," said the psalmist. Heartaches can breed bitterness, resentment, and self-pity, and we become like a stagnant swamp. When you are hurt, the temptation is to complain. But when your heart is trusting in Him, the resulting song in your heart will dry your tears.

20

WHEN YOU ARE AGITATED

Abbé Pierre has a phrase, "penicillin for despair." He declares that to be the world's greatest need. I am inclined to agree. Every person who has been plagued by anxious fears feels the need of "penicillin for despair." Certainly Christ felt that need.

As He knelt that night in Gethsemane, the Bible says, "He . . . began to be sore amazed, and to be very heavy" (Mark 14:33). The Revised Version translates that to read, "He . . . began to be greatly distressed and troubled." Moffatt's translation gives this, "He began to feel appalled and agitated."

In commenting on this, Leslie Weatherhead quotes Vincent Taylor, the world-famous Greek scholar, who says, "Those verbs denote distress which follows a great shock." He points out that hundreds and thousands of British people are still suffering from the shock of the last war, though many of them do not realize it. There are many in America still suffering from the shock of that war. And there are numerous other shocks which have come into the personal lives of people.

I have had many people tell me that when they go to bed they toss and turn for hours before sleep comes. Others have told how they would suddenly begin trembling, or break into a cold sweat, or feel constant fatigue, or have an abnormal dryness in the mouth, or a constant headache, or a palpitating heart. Some describe a deadness of feeling when they seemed to lose ability to love their own families, or even God. Some have told me about inclinations to suicide.

For people who know the suffering brought by anxious fears, I have deep sympathy. I have had some of those same feelings. Nearly every normal person has at some time been very heavy—greatly distressed—troubled—appalled—agitated. Some people seem condemned to live with an anxiety neurosis as a constant companion.

In times of anxious strain we are told to "have faith" and all our troubles will magically disappear. That is simply not true. Jesus had faith but He also knew the meaning of naked terror. Some of the greatest saints have cried out for "penicillin for despair," yet they also had faith.

We are told that our fears are imaginary. That is a misstatement. All fears are real—none are imaginary. It may be that imagination causes our fears, or it may be that we react in the wrong way to some circumstance of life, but fears are not imaginary. We are told to "pull ourselves together," but we are not sure what that means. Many do not feel they have strength enough to pull even if they knew what to pull on.

When we have a certain type of infection, the physician gives us penicillin and soon the infection is gone. There is a penicillin for despair.

When you feel despair, or deep anxiety, or trembling fear, or nervous strain—what attitude should you take toward it? Examine the experience of Christ when He felt "very heavy" (Mark 14:32–36).

We know that Christ was God and that as God He had supernatural insight and power. But also Christ was man; and as man He experienced our same hungers and thirsts; He endured temptation that was real; He had human desires; He had experiences of deep anxiety and despair.

Thus we know that anxious fears may come even though one does have faith, and we should not feel ashamed because of nervous symptoms generated by these experiences. But we must remember that there is such a thing as "penicillin for despair." It isn't a pill or a shot in the arm; it is an action or a series of actions. In His moment of despair, Christ did these three things:

(1) He got alone. That night in Gethsemane He moved a distance from the crowd and took with Him His three closest friends. There are times when it is good for us to be with crowds. There are other times when we need to be with some trusted and close friends. Jesus no doubt talked with these about His troubles, and often that helps. It is wonderful to have a friend to share our deepest thoughts. Often it helps to talk with a minister or a competent counselor. But then Jesus went further on alone. It is important to see this.

When one is in some dark valley, his first impulse is to tell his troubles to every person who will listen. The reason we want to tell our troubles is because we want sympathy, we get satisfaction from the pity of others and from self-pity. We may deny this but it is true.

127

The more we talk about our troubles, the worse they may become. Speech has a much greater effect on the emotions than thinking. We can talk ourselves into almost anything. Jesus got alone.

(2) Jesus looked up to God. He said, "Father, all things are possible unto thee." He took His mind off Himself, and that does much to relieve one of anxiety and fear. But often this is hard to do because part of the mind wants to hold on to its worries and despair. That is the easiest way out. To despair is to lose hope and to lose hope is to be able to give up and to quit.

Frequently we translate our despair into bodily illness. Maybe we don't become invalids but we never "feel well." Much sickness is merely an escape from reality. It is the easiest way out, but it is never a final solution. Deep down we are ashamed of our cowardice. We feel guilty for selling our courage to buy sympathy.

When one looks into the face of God, he has hope because he knows that "all things are possible unto him."

(3) Jesus took positive action. When He "began to be sore amazed, and to be very heavy"—that is, distressed, troubled, and despairing—He went to a place alone, He looked into the face of God, and He took positive action.

In the midst of despair, the great temptation is to retire, to slip into illness, to surrender. It is a great struggle to do something. It was a struggle for our Lord. Luke vividly portrays the strain Christ was under, saying, ". . . his sweat was as it were great drops of blood falling down to the ground" (Luke 22:24). But in spite of the struggle, Jesus centered His mind on something to do. He refused to retire into Himself.

Activity is often the best cure for the blues. As previously mentioned, physicians tell us that our fear thoughts come from the higher brain centers while physical activity comes from the lower brain centers. When one begins to exercise those lower brain centers through activity, it lessens the tension on the upper brain centers. Operations are performed where certain parts of the brain are removed to lessen those fear thoughts. I knew a man who took daily exercise. He said it "straightened out his thoughts."

What did Jesus do? He prayed, ". . . not my will, but thine, be done." He wholly committed Himself to the will of God. There is the faith that is the answer to fear. It lifts one's thoughts away from his own troubles and centers his mind on the strength of God.

"In His will is our peace" is the "penicillin for despair." Commitment to His will cures despair and brings peace by taking from us the fear of getting lost; by relieving us of the burden of the responsibility of tomorrow; by giving us the approval of a good conscience; by giving us a constructive life to live. Dedication to His will enables us to say with the psalmist, "Yea, though I walk through the valley of the shadow of death, I will fear no evil: for thou art with me." Realizing that He is with us, we have confidence that we will get through even the worst experience. Thus there is no room in our minds for despair.

Here is a little poem that expresses it well:

Worry? Why worry? What can worry do?
It never keeps a trouble from overtaking you.
It gives you indigestion and sleepless hours at night
And fills with gloom the days, however fair and bright.

It puts a frown upon the face, and sharpness to the tone
We're unfit to live with others and unfit to live alone
Worry? Why worry? What can worry do?
It never keeps a trouble from overtaking you.

Pray? Why pray? What can praying do?
Praying really changes things, arranges life anew.
It's good for your digestion, gives peaceful sleep at night
And fills the grayest, gloomiest day—with rays of glowing
   light.

It puts a smile upon your face, the love note in your tone
Makes you fit to live with others, and fit to live alone.
Pray? Why pray? What can praying do?
It brings God down from heaven, to live and work with you.

21

PRAYING FOR OTHERS

During the Last Supper, Jesus turned and said, "Simon, Simon . . . I have prayed for thee" (Luke 22:31, 32). And again and again we have followed our Lord's example. One day I was visiting a dear mother upon whom the years were now resting heavily. Not only was she old and feeble; her body for several years had been burdened with great pain.

She turned to me and asked, "Why do you suppose God is keeping me here?" I didn't know and so I made no reply. Then she began telling me about her son. He had missed the way and was living a life that was wrong. As she told me about him, I thought of the words of the poem, "I know whose love would follow me still, mother o' mine." In spite of her disappointment in him and the fact that he had repeatedly broken her heart, she still held on to him. Finally she answered her own question: "God is keeping me here to pray for my son."

Many times we feel so helpless—that loved one is beyond our reach, someone is desperately sick, some situation seems hopeless—but we can always pray. Not only is prayer for others our privilege, it is our solemn duty. The prophet Samuel said, ". . . God forbid that I should sin against the LORD in ceasing to pray for you . . ." (1 Sam. 12:23). The Christian prays for loved ones. Also, the Christian prays for those who are hard to love. Jesus commands, ". . . pray for them which despitefully use you, and persecute you" (Matt. 5:44).

Praying for another person helps in many ways. It helps the person who prays. A man spoke to me the other day about another man who had done him a great wrong. Rather defiantly he said, "Don't preach to me about forgiveness. I can't forgive him and even if I could, I wouldn't." I said, "I only ask you to do one thing. Call that man's name in your prayers until something happens. If you want him punished, ask God to do it." I quoted to him the Scripture. "Vengeance is mine; I will repay, saith the Lord" (Rom. 12:19).

When we talk to God about "that other person," eventually the hot fires of hate in our soul will be put out and we will begin to look at that person in the spirit of Him who said, "Father, forgive them." When we pray about some loved one who needs help, we develop a spirit of hope and optimism that is a sustaining strength in our own lives. When your child is sick, you feel a great sense of relief when the doctor comes because you know he can do something. And when you lift someone who needs help into the hands of God, you feel peace in your own heart. Praying for someone else helps you.

When Jesus said, "Simon, I have prayed for thee," that brought great encouragement to Simon. When the great Martin Luther felt particularly strong and happy, he would exclaim, "I feel as if I were being prayed for." When a person is under criticism by someone else, it pushes him down further. But when he knows there is someone praying for him, that very knowledge is a source of sustaining strength.

Once during a difficult time in England's history, Cromwell wrote his admirals at sea: "You have a plentiful stock of prayers going up for you daily, which is to us and I trust to you, a matter of great encouragement." I know a lot of people who are praying for me, and to each one I am deeply grateful.

Recently some people in another church were telling me some of the faults of their pastor. I told them of how St. Paul asked his churches to pray for him. In fact, he asked for prayers in every letter he wrote, except to the backslidden church of Galatia. I could name preachers whose effectiveness has been measurably increased when they learned of people in their churches praying regularly for them.

It helps anyone to know somebody is praying for him or her.

When I pray for another person, it inspires me to do what I can to help that person. And quite often the effort of the person praying is enough to answer the prayer. For example, suppose I pray for someone who is sick. It may be that a contributing factor in that sickness is that the sick person is lonely, discouraged, and has lost the will to live. As a result of my praying, I am moved to acts of thoughtfulness and kindness which may change my friend's mental attitude, and that may be the turning point between illness and health.

If I pray for someone who is in financial need, I am inspired to share my own resources with that one. If I pray about the soul of a person I will be moved to invite him to my church with me. If I pray about my community's welfare, I will give more time in community service.

When I pray for another person, I bring the power of God to bear upon that person's life and situation. The Bible says: "Is any sick among you? let him call for the elders of the church; and let them pray over him . . . And the prayer of faith shall save the sick, and the Lord shall raise him up; and if he have committed sins, they shall be forgiven him . . . pray one for another . . ." (James 5:14–16).

Notice especially that phrase, "the prayer of faith." We know that faith is the very foundation of prayer but here we see that it is not always necessary for the person prayed for to have faith. God can answer the prayer because of the faith of the person praying. I may pray for someone who has no faith, but if I pray a prayer of faith, God can answer it.

On the cross Jesus prayed, "Father, forgive them . . ." (Luke 23:34). Certainly Jesus would not have prayed an impossible prayer. He knew that those who crucified Him were not repentant and had no faith, yet God could forgive them on the basis of the prayer that was prayed for them.

Have you prayed for someone and yet the answer has not come? Every sincere prayer should include the words of Christ, ". . . nevertheless not my will, but thine, be done," and it may be that the answer you asked for is not according to God's will.

Or it may be that for some reason God has delayed the answer to your prayer. Let us remember the words of the psalmist, "Delight thyself also in the LORD; and he shall give thee the desires of thine heart. Commit thy way unto the LORD; trust also in him; and he shall bring it to pass . . . Rest in the LORD, and wait patiently for him . . ." (Ps. 37:4, 5, 7).

But it may be that you have not prayed in the right way. I have given much study to the method of prayer and I am convinced that some get answers more completely than others simply because they know better how to pray. Let me put down for you my own method of praying for another person:

First, pray definitely for that one person. Get that person clearly in your mind so that you can see, him or her vividly. Decide as definitely as you can the need of that person, considering the circumstances of his or her life.

Second, holding that particular person in mind, think of God. It helps me to think of some particular scene in the life of Christ that may apply to this situation. For example, if the person has physical needs, think of Christ feeding the five thousand; if the person is living wrongly, think of Him saying to that fallen one, "Go and sin no more"; if the person is sick, think of the woman who touched the hem of His garment. Now, you are thinking of God and the particular person together.

Third, think of your prayer as lifting that person into the presence of God. You are not trying to tell God something He does not know. Neither are you trying to persuade God to do something He doesn't want to do. Realize, as Augustine said, "Without God, we cannot; without us, God will not." Think of yourself as supplying the human co-operation that is necessary to bring the person and God together.

Fourth, tell God what is on your heart. Remember, however, to pray positively. Don't concentrate on the person's weakness, sickness, or wrong. Rather, concentrate on the person's strengths and picture in your mind the answer you want and picture that person receiving that answer. Thus, you pray hopefully.

Fifth, keep praying until God's answer comes.

In the year 1872, Professor John Tyndall, a British scientist, declared that prayer is of no value. In defense of his position, he challenged the Christian people to a test. He said: "Go into a hospital ward and divide the patients into two equal groups. Make sure that they have similar illnesses and that they receive the same medical attention, but let Christian people pray for one

group and neglect the other. Then we shall see if any improve-
ment is shown in the patients who have been prayed for."

To begin with, that experiment would be completely impossible. You could not divide sick people into two groups suffering
from illnesses of identical severity. Neither could you be sure that
each group received identical medical care. But more important,
you could not be certain that some in the "neglected" group were
not being prayed for by some loved one.

But, if the experiment could be carried out, it would prove
beyond a shadow of a doubt that prayer makes a difference.
Prayer is effective not only in reference to sick people; it has the
power to meet every need in life. Time and again, I have suggested to a wife or a husband whose marriage was not happy,
"Without telling the other one, pray earnestly every day about
it." Many times I have seen prayer work when everything else
had failed.

A lady phoned me the other day asking if I knew the name
of a minister in Los Angeles. She told me of her brother there
who needed God's help and she wanted that minister to pray for
him. I said, "Why don't you and I pray for him?" "Oh, he's too
far away for that," she replied. I then pointed out to her that I
could dial the long-distance operator and in a matter of moments
I could be talking with that man. That is made possible through
the power of electricity.

Then I pointed out that God created electricity and, if by it
my voice can be carried across the continent, it is just as rea-
sonable to believe that God can take my prayer and send it anywhere. Frequently I think of the little poem:

If radio's slim fingers can pluck a melody
From night—and toss it over a continent or sea;
If the petalled white notes of a violin

136

Are blown across the mountains or the city's din;
If songs, like crimson roses, are culled from thin blue air—
Why should mortals wonder if God hears prayer?

—Ethel Romig Fuller[2]

Picture some person in one room of a house and God in the next room. Between the two there is a wall. But if you stand in the doorway connecting the two rooms, then you can see the ones in each room. One could speak to the other through you. It may be that you have contact with some person who needs God's help. Between that person and God there may be a wall of unbelief, or unconcern, or wrong living. But because you have contact both with that person and with God, you become the contact between the two and your prayers connect that person's need with God's power. That is intercessory prayer.

22

PRAYING FOR HEALING

The Bible emphasizes the power of faith. To gain healing and health through faith and prayer, one must follow four essential steps:

(1) Substantial belief that God can and will heal.

(2) Belief in the combined use of medical science and religious faith.

(3) Removal of the spiritual hindrances to healing such as sin and wrong attitudes.

(4) Acceptance of God's will for our lives and of His answer to our prayers.

Let us consider these four steps.

(1) The Bible says, ". . . he that cometh to God must believe that he is, and that he is a rewarder of them that diligently seek him" (Heb. 11:6). Either there is a God or there is not a God. If there is a God, either He can effectively use His power in our minds and bodies or He cannot. If God can, then He will either hear and answer our prayers or He will not.

Either you do believe or you do not believe. We recall the father who brought his sick son to Christ. He said, ". . . if thou canst do any thing. . . ." But the Master corrected him, "If thou canst believe . . ." (Mark 9:22, 23). The "if" is not in reference to God—the "if" is with us. It all depends on whether or not we believe.

No person believes perfectly, neither does any person doubt completely. Within every one of us is both belief and doubt. The question is, which do we hold before us? If you will begin by emphasizing your belief, by practicing what faith you have, it will grow. You believe something about God; what is it? That is the place for you to begin.

(2) To send for the physician, to go to the hospital, is not an expression of lack of faith in God. On the contrary, we believe God works both through physical laws and through spiritual laws. The physician understands the construction of the human body and how it operates. He also understands the nature of physical sickness, its causes, and its cures.

Of course, the knowledge of the physician is not complete. He has much to learn; here is the importance of medical research. But God made the physician and God made all the medicines; and through their proper use many of our prayers for healing are being answered. How God answers is not as important as the fact that He does answer.

However, there are factors in healing that go far beyond medical science. When I talk with God about a sick person, my first

139

prayer is for the physician and the nurses, that they may be open channels of God's healing grace. But beyond the operation of the physical laws and their applications is the operation of the spiritual laws of God. The practice of faith is just as scientific and real as is the practice of medicine.

I am certain that faith can and does work miracles and that in many, many cases, faith is the difference which tips the scales in favor of healing and health and against death or incurable illness.

(3) In considering the use of faith in healing and health, not only must we emphasize our belief and recognize the relationship between the practice of medicine and the practice of faith, but our lives must be cleansed of those things which block God's spirit from our lives.

I have enjoyed some correspondence with Harold Sherman. He wrote some complimentary things about my book, *God's Psychiatry*. But better is his book *Your Key to Happiness*. He has a lot to say about the relationship of how a man thinks and how he feels. And a fine example comes out of his own experience.

He was engaged to revise an important radio presentation with the promise that he would be given a contract for a permanent job. After months of hard work, he was dismissed and his material used without credit to him. This resulted in both financial difficulty for him and humiliation. He grew so bitter that he actually had murder in his heart.

He developed an infection in his throat. He had the best medical attention but it was to no avail. Later, he became willing to surrender his hate, to pray for those who had wronged him, to both forgive and be forgiven; only then did his throat condition heal.

Study some of the words of our language. For example, notice the resemblance between the words "meditation" and "medication." If you will study it further, you will find that meditation upon God is truly medication for one's body. Consider the words "wholeness" and "holiness." One means complete health, the other means complete sinlessness. The two go together.

As someone has put it:

> He who formed our frame
> Made man a perfect whole
> And made the body's health
> Depend upon the soul.

(4) As in the case of all prayer, we must accept the will of God and His answer. Why is it that prayer brings healing to one person but not to another? "The prayer of faith shall save the sick." It may be that our prayers were ineffective through lack of faith or because we did not know how to pray. Prayer is a science to be studied and learned and some people are far more powerful in prayer than are others. On the other hand, healing may not be God's will under the circumstances. Certainly for each person there comes a time for this mortal life to end. Otherwise, the blessed immortality would be forever denied us.

But we have every reason to believe God's will is health instead of sickness, strength instead of weakness, pleasure instead of pain. Surely He does not enjoy seeing His children suffer. And when we believe in Him and pray with faith, when we do all we can within our power to use the means of health available to us, when we surrender our wrongs and open the way for His cleansing and forgiving love, and above all, when we trust His wisdom in the answer, then a marvelous peace will be about us and in us. A peace that eliminates our fear, our panic. Then the promise of the psalmist is fulfilled for us, "Wait on the LORD: be of good courage, and he shall strengthen thine heart . . ." (27:14).

141

As I write this I can see a man out in the garden raking up the leaves. It makes me sad. I think I have never enjoyed the leaves more than this autumn.

My study has large windows on three sides and through those windows I can see up and down lovely Fairview Road in Atlanta. Surely the trees are no more colorful anywhere and their beautiful profusion of autumn color has been food for my soul. It was Charles Kingsley who called beauty "God's handwriting"; and seeing the beauty of the trees, I do not see how any person in his right mind can fail to believe in God.

But now the leaves have lost their beauty and it seems the trees are saying, "There is no use for me to hold on to you any longer." One by one the leaves fall to the ground to become nothing but trash. So the man comes to rake them up to be burned or carried away by the garbage collector to some dumping place. The trees are left bare and ugly, like skeletons.

Thinking of this has brought to mind a shocking statement I read about God. This writer said, "There is a sense in which we ought to think of God as a Celestial Garbage Collector." That seems a terrible thing to say. However, the writer went on to explain that life could not be kept pure and clean without God. Things in our lives that were beautiful were somehow allowed to die and one by one we dropped them. But to get rid of our broken dreams, our soiled ideals, our stained consciences, is not so easy. They become garbage in our lives with a stench in our nostrils.

Dr. Henry Sloane Coffin was in China talking to a group of native Christian preachers. He said, "Tell me what it was about the Christian faith that won you from the other faiths?" Was it the miracles? No, they had miracles in their own religion. Was it Christ's teaching? No, their own teachers said wonderful things.

Finally one of the elderly men said, "It was Jesus washing His disciples' feet." The others all agreed that was it. God, stooping down with a towel and a wash basin. And even more wonderful is how He looks upon our sins, the sins we are willing to turn loose and let go, and how He takes them away—but He doesn't stop there.

As I look at the trees, my mind runs months ahead. Now they are bare, but after winter comes the spring. On the limbs of the tree will burst forth new life, bringing buds and blossoms and fruit and more leaves. The tree will become beautiful and appealing again. It will feel no shame as men gaze upon it; proudly it will stretch itself toward the heavens and stand straight and tall.

He is more, much more, than a "Celestial Garbage Collector"—He is the one who said, ". . . I am come that they might have life, and that they might have it more abundantly" (John 10:10). Under His power, we receive a new chance at life. Surely we can believe that God, who does that for the trees, would do no less for His own children.

23

THE PRAYER OF FAITH
THAT SAVES THE SICK

There is a wonderful promise of healing in the Bible: "And the prayer of faith shall save the sick, and the Lord shall raise him up . . ." (James 5:15). Because sooner or later every person is deeply concerned with sickness, either in himself or in some loved one, that verse interests us. To understand it, there are several things to be said.

Note, the word used is "save" instead of "heal." God's saving of the sick may include healing, but not in every case. He does not always promise healing, but if faith is exercised, God does always promise saving which is much more important. Often it is that sickness is used by God to create faith.

One of the world's greatest comedians was Sir Harry Lauder. One day the news came that his son had been killed. Of course he was shocked to the depths of his soul. After he had been able to think this tragedy through, he said: "In a time like this there are three courses open to a man: (1) He may give way to despair, sour upon the world and become a grouch. (2) He may endeavor to drown his sorrows in drink or by a life of waywardness and wickedness. (3) He may turn to God." Sir Harry took that third course and, though God did not heal his sorrow by returning his son to him, that sorrow became the instrument by which he found God, developed his faith, and found life's greatest meanings. He kept the pain but gained the power to endure the pain, and that in itself is a high form of healing.

Think of Luther Burbank. As a boy he was a semi-invalid. Because of his sickness, his days and nights were filled with the fear that his life would be a complete failure. He worked in a hot, dusty factory in New England but finally the place where his health could stand it no longer. He was forced to work outdoors. He got a job working with plants and flowers. Eventually he became the greatest naturalist of all time. It was Burbank who said, "Every weed can be made a flower," and he showed how it could be done. Certainly he learned faith but had it not been for his sickness, he would have spent his life in a factory. Because of his sickness he learned faith, and surely it led to his saving.

There is A. J. Cronin, who was a very successful physician in London. Sickness forced him to lose his practice and move into the country. At first he was bitter and resentful but gradually faith began to grow within him. Later he began to write and as a result, we have such books as *The Citadel, The Keys of the Kingdom,* and others.

There were two brothers who were sickly as children. Their home knew sickness almost constantly. Gradually they began to develop faith in the idea that sickness could be healed and, as a result of their faith, they gave themselves to the task. They were the Mayo brothers. Sickness led to their saving.

145

There is an important point to see here. Sickness may lead to panic, resentment, and resignation. On the contrary, sickness may lead to a calm look at one's own life, to faith, and to dedication to a higher purpose. And if through sickness, one is led to faith, then that faith in some way leads to the saving of the person. When we are on our backs, we find it much easier to look up.

The "saving" may take the form of healing. One of the most respected ministers in the world today is Dr. Leslie D. Weatherhead of London. His book *Psychology, Religion, and Healing* is a fine study of divine healing.

He gives many actual cases of healing by faith. For example, there was a nurse who was very sick in the hospital. Her temperature was very high, she had not taken any food for some days; she was unconscious. She could not know anyone was praying for her. In the church service one night, Dr. Weatherhead asked the congregation to pray for her. He said, "Believe that at this very moment Christ is touching her life, and that His healing power is being made manifest in her body now."

After a few moments of silence, he said, "Please do not let your minds wander. Hold them steadily there, lifting up this girl to God." It was later found that during that very hour her temperature went down to normal, she slept naturally without drugs, the next morning she took light food and within days had made a marvelous recovery.

Or healing may be of another type. Some time ago I went to speak in a large factory. Afterwards the superintendent showed me through the place and explained to me their operation. There were several hundred women machine operators there. They ran those machines so fast one's eyes could hardly follow the movement of their hands.

As we walked along I was startled to see that one of those women had no fingers on her left hand. I looked again and saw no fingers on her right hand. I said to the superintendent, "Can that girl do this work?" He said, "She is one of the most accurate and fastest machine operators we have." On her face was a smile and I am sure in her heart was a song.

That girl is a clear case of divine healing. In that community the only jobs available for women involved running a machine. But she had no fingers. She likely had faith enough to pray to God for fingers. And He could miraculously have given them to her. Of that I have no doubt. Instead, God healed her in another way. He gave her the power to accomplish her dreams of a job in spite of her lack of fingers. She became healed in that her handicap ceased to be a handicap.

So it was with St. Paul. Three times he prayed God to remove the thorn in his flesh. Instead of removing it, God gave him the strength to bear it (2 Cor. 12:7–9). That is healing. And when we are sick in body, mind, or heart, God may not take away the pain. Instead, He may give us a quality of character that overcomes our self-pity, despair, or complaining, and makes us know that life can still be a triumphant experience.

Faith always wins victories but in a variety of ways. Faith is never defeated.

You are familiar with the work of Dr. Harvey Cushing, a truly great brain specialist. One of his patients wrote: "I knew quite well I was going mad. Nearly five years of war service followed by an immediate plunge into disastrous commercial affairs had brought me to the end of my strength. When my wife said Dr. Cushing would see me, I said, 'What's the use? Another blasted doctor can't help me.'"

However, the man did go to see the doctor. Dr. Cushing looked him straight in the eye. He had never been looked at so intensely before or since. After examinations the doctor spoke, "You came here thinking I'd send you to a madhouse. Forget it.

You are all right. You are suffering from suppressed war shock aggravated by chronic overwork and worry, but you are as sane as I am. If you go out of here believing the truth I am telling you, you will be all right in a year. If you leave thinking I am jollying you along, then you won't live. I hope you will believe me."

The man later reported, "I believed him. He was sure, and he made me know he was sure; above all was the sense of the man's innate goodness and greatness. I went into his presence a tottering wreck; I left him confident and happy." That man was healed, but what healed him? It was his faith in Dr. Cushing. And, if faith in a mere man has that power to heal, how much greater is the power of faith in the eternal God?

You remember the father who brought his sick son to Christ (Mark 9:14–27). The first thing the Master did was to assure the man of His interest. He asked, "How long is it ago since this came unto him?" That is, "I want to know about the boy; I am glad to listen." That is the first step to faith in God. Unless we believe God cares enough to listen, we can never have faith.

Next, Jesus draws out what faith the man has. He says, "If thou canst believe, all things are possible. . . ." Next we read, ". . . the father of the child cried out, and said with tears. . . ." Those tears are manly and precious. You cannot approach God on irreverent, flippant feet. Faith is never found until we are deadly serious about it. The father said, ". . . I believe; help thou mine unbelief." That is, "My belief is not perfect. I still have some unbeliefs—some doubts." That father had prayed so many times and been disappointed. He didn't claim a faith he did not possess, but he still was willing to use what faith he had. He was both honest and humble, although he was cynical.

Jesus did heal the boy. Later his disciples wanted to know why they couldn't heal him. The Lord replied, "This kind can come forth by nothing, but by prayer and fasting." Fasting doesn't mean going without something to eat. It means an emptying process, the turning loose those things contrary to the Spirit of God. Prayer is consecration to God, to His will and purposes. And that is the process through which faith comes.

As James said, "The prayer of faith shall save." Not only the sick in reference to physical illness, but the sick in any life situation. Claim that promise of God.

24

HOW GOD ANSWERS
PRAYER

Have you had an answer to prayer? I asked that question in my newspaper column, but I did not expect the number of replies I got. In fact, it took me about a week to read them all. As I read the many letters I received, I was first impressed by the fact that "God is no respecter of persons."

Some replies came on the letterheads of prominent businessmen, others on the cheapest tablet paper, written with pencil. Some of the letters were from people who gave me the impression of being well educated and cultured, others were from people who could express themselves only with great difficulty. Through some of the letters there were revealed qualities of a saintly life which has been lived close to God; others told me of how they had sinned and were ashamed of their lives.

But when it comes to prayer, we all stand on equal ground and each has the right of access to the Father. The learned and the unlearned, the rich and the poor, the saint and the sinner, all stand in need before God; and when in prayer they carry that need to God, He answers. Jesus said, "For everyone that asketh receiveth . . ." (Matt. 7:8), and when He said "every one," He meant just that.

Also, I was deeply impressed with the complete sincerity of those who wrote me. In belittling prayer, some claim that so-called answers are mere coincidence, that the prayer made no difference; but many, many people believe that prayer is what did make the difference. And it is awfully hard to argue with one who has prayed and to whom the answer has come.

In some instances, the answer came through God showing the person praying what to do. One wrote: "I wanted so much to do something for the Chinzei Gakuin Nagasaki School in Japan. Many of the teachers and students were killed by the atom bomb. But I had no money to give. I prayed God to show me something I could do. A few days later I saw an item in the *Wesleyan Christian Advocate* requesting copies of the *National Geographic Magazine* for this school. My father had taken this magazine for many years and the old copies were in my possession. I was so glad to send them. It was an answer to my prayer. The principal, the Reverend Taneo Chiba, seems very grateful for the magazines."

A dear lady of eighty-two years wrote that after an operation she was told she could never walk again. "The next morning I told my nurse I was getting up and if I fell I knew the Lord would catch me. My nurse said I mustn't do that but I said, 'Get out of my way,' and I did walk and have been walking now for five years. Praise God from whom all blessings flow." That reminds me of the Lord saying to one, "Rise, take up thy bed, and walk"

(John 5:8). A lot of people could walk in many ways if they just had the faith and spirit of that lady. She thinks prayer gave her what she needed.

In response to my request for answers to prayer there came many replies showing how God often works through people. One wrote: "A retired minister's wife who lives near me is very helpful to a little neighbor girl. Her parents are poor and I noticed last Sunday at church that the little girl needed some better clothes.

"I told the minister's wife that I wanted to give her the money to buy the little girl some things. She almost broke into tears and said, 'Before coming today, I prayed that someone would help buy the clothes the little girl needed.' Some other ladies heard the conversation and they also gave and now the little girl has all she needs."

Would you say that God put it into the heart of that woman to notice the child's clothes and to want to give to her? That lady who gave and the one who prayed believe it was prayer that made the difference. I do, too.

Through the years I have read much about mental telepathy, thought transference, and the like. Among the answers to prayer were many somewhat in that category. For example, this one: "At times I was troubled about my son who was away during World War II. When that feeling came over me, I would stop whatever I was doing, kneel, and ask God to be very near to my boy. One day I wrote him asking if there were times when it seemed he could not go on and then he would, for no apparent reason, feel a lot better and feel peace and comfort in his heart. He wrote he had had that experience many times. Then I knew God had answered my prayers."

Another wrote: "One of my sons had been ill for some time and had failed to let me hear from him. I became very much distressed and became more and more anxious about him. Finally

I reached the point I felt I could stand it no longer. Since I did not know how to get in touch with him by phone, I knelt and pleaded with God to 'let a letter come to me in the next mail.' I arose and got into my bed. Just then the phone rang. It was my sick son. He said, 'Mama, I have you so strongly on my mind tonight that I just had to call.' God heard and answered my prayer." Did that boy just happen to think of calling his mother or was he prompted by some higher power?

Does God guide us directly in the making of certain decisions? One wrote: "I was confronted with a problem. Something came up that I did not want to do, yet I wanted God's will done. I decided to go into the living room, get on my knees, and ask God to make it plain to me if I should do this thing or not. I seemed to receive no answer and presently got up to leave the room. As I touched the door knob, I clearly heard a voice saying, 'Do it, do it, do it.' My burden was lifted and I found it easy to do what I then knew He wanted me to do."

Concerning the matter of answers to prayer, one wrote: "You remember the story in the Bible of Eli and little Samuel, how God spoke to the boy telling him what to do. Well, I made up my mind that if God spoke to little Samuel, He would speak to me. We had gone to Miami to live. A man offered us a chance to share with him in buying an apartment house. It looked like a grand opportunity.

"My mother, husband, and brother thought it a wonderful buy and they insisted. I made up my mind to pray and ask God what to do. I sat there praying, listening for God's voice. The others wanted to know why I hesitated, it seemed such a good proposition. God's voice did come. He said not to buy. The ones who did invest lost everything."

To some that story may sound almost ridiculous. Yet, I personally know some very successful businessmen who never make a move until first they have prayed and sought the guidance of God.

Many of the letters I received about prayer answers were in regard to sickness and healing. This is something I believe in very strongly. Never a day goes by that I do not pray definitely for certain ones who are sick, and I could fill a book with answers I have received. The many letters from others along this line served to strengthen my own faith.

One man wrote: "I have just returned home from a hospital where I suffered a severe heart attack a few weeks ago. After I was well enough to have visitors, my little nine-year-old granddaughter came to see me with her parents. As they were leaving she turned and came back to my bedside and said to me, 'Granddaddy, do you know why you got better?' I answered her, 'No, why?' Then she said, 'It was because I prayed so hard for you to get well.'"

Do you believe a little nine-year-old girl's prayer made any difference? There is a granddaddy in Georgia who believes God heard a little girl and answered her prayer.

Another wrote about a strong fear of a forthcoming operation. "I prayed to God to guide the knife, and guide the man's mind that was to hold the knife, and stay close to my side all through the operation. I asked God to take complete charge of me and whatever the outcome was I would be satisfied, because I knew that He knew what was best.

"I gave the whole matter, including myself, to Him, and I said, 'Here I am, Lord. If it's your will for me to live, I'll live. If it's your will for me to die, I'll die.' Right then, that moment, the heaviness of my heart, that terrible fear, that whole burden was lifted from me. And immediately I felt His presence. I know He was there. He had heard my prayer."

It is quite possible that the peace and calm that came into that one's heart made the difference between life and death. God, in that case, worked through the physician, but the physician needed the cooperation of the patient. God's answer to prayer made that possible.

Answers to prayer are thrilling to study. Especially do I like this one: "My son was instantly killed in an automobile accident, leaving a young wife. She was so heartbroken that it seemed she would have a complete collapse. We all did our best to help her but nothing helped.

"I began praying for God to please send another to take my son's place in her heart. God did answer that prayer. God did send a young man into her life and immediately her heartaches began to turn into happiness. They married and now have a little son. They are as happy as can be and this has made her parents and me happy. I know God heard my prayers and made it possible for these two young people to meet."

I have heard it said, "Marriages are made in heaven." Some of them seem to be, anyway.

Another wrote: "I want to tell you about the answer to my most fervent prayer that took four long years to come. I have a wonderful little boy. When he was a year old, we wanted another child so that the two could grow together. Not long after our little boy's first birthday, we learned the wonderful news that we were to have another child. Imagine our heartbreak and disappointment when we lost it a few months later.

"That was only the first of our disappointments, for in the next three years I lost two more babies. All during that time I kept praying God would give us another child. Each night I prayed with all the sincerity of my soul. But gradually I began to wonder if I were not being a little selfish. We did have one child and I knew some that had not had that blessing. Then I began

155

to pray, 'Not my will, but Thine be done.' And I suddenly knew my sense of despair was gone. I asked God to guide my life according to His plan.

"Perhaps it was the willingness to accept something other than my greatest desire that brought the answer to my prayer; for two weeks after our son's fifth birthday, a beautiful baby boy was born to us. I truly believe God answered my prayer, and I thank Him every night for His blessings to us."

Sometimes God does say, "Wait." Maybe He has to wait until we are ready for His answer and through prayer we do become ready.

I don't understand prayer anymore than I understand electricity. But I do know that man builds a generator that catches out of the air that marvelous power, electricity, and we use that power to do so many things for us. God made electricity and I believe the God who made a power to light our homes did not forget to make a power to light up our lives. The God who made a power to pull our trains did not forget to make a power to help His children along the way of life. Prayer is the means by which we obtain God's power. Lord, teach us to pray!

NOTES

1. From "Preview of the Next 25 Years," article condensed from *Fortune* (January, 1955), copyright by Time, Inc.

2. "Proof," copyright 1931 by Ethel Romig Fuller, quoted by her permission.

Oct. 24, 2016